U.S. History

and

Government

Ten Day Competency Review

Authors:

Paul Stich
Wappingers Central Schools
Wappingers Falls, New York

Susan F. Pingel
Skaneateles Central Schools
Skaneateles, New York

John Farrell
New York Archdiocesan Schools
Cardinal Spellman High School, Bronx, NY

Editors:

Wayne Garnsey and Paul Stich
Wappingers Central Schools
Wappingers Falls, New York

Cover Design, Illustrations, and Artwork:

Eugene B. Fairbanks
Granville, New York

N & N Publishing Company, Inc.
18 Montgomery Street   Middletown, New York 10940
(914) 342 - 1677

Dedicated to our students, with the sincere hope that
U.S. History and Government — Ten Day Competency Review
will further enhance their education and better prepare them
with an appreciation and understanding of the people
and historical events that have shaped our world.

Special Credits

Thanks to the many teachers who have contributed their knowledge, skills,
and years of experience to the making of our 10 Day Review.

To these educators, our sincere thanks
for their assistance in the preparation of this manuscript:

Cindy Fairbanks
Kenneth Garnsey
Anne McCabe
William Schlink
Victor Salamone
Gloria Tonkinson

Special thanks to our understanding families.

U.S. History and Government — Ten Day Competency Review
was produced on the Apple Macintosh II and Apple LaserMax 1000.
MacWrite II by Claris and *Canvas* by Deneba were used to produce
text, graphics, and illustrations. Original line drawings were repro-
duced with *VersaScan* on a Microtek MS-300A scanner and modified
with *DeskPaint* by Zedcor. The format, special designs, graphic incor-
poration, and page layout were accomplished with *Ready Set Go* by
Manhattan Graphics.
    Special technical assistance was provided by Frank Valenza and Len
Genesee of *Computer Productions*, Newburgh, New York.

*To all, thank you for your excellent software, hardware, and your
technical support.*

SAN # 216-4221   ISBN # 0935487-54-9

Printed in the United States of America

Revised
3/1/94

4567890 BMP 0987654

Table of Contents

To The Student

This book has been written and designed by experienced Social Studies teachers to help you prepare for a Competency Test in United States History and Government.

Often, students lose more points on written competency questions than they do on the multiple choice questions. We believe this is because they do not understand the requirements of these questions and they leave sections out or do not give facts to support their general ideas.

The eight lessons and practice exam of this book will help you overcome these problems.

The eight lessons deal with the concepts and issues appearing frequently on the test. Each of the eight lessons has background readings and exercises, multiple choice questions, and a model essay.

On the model essay, we stress using the pre-writing exercise. It will help you

- to see all the parts of the question you need

- to write important facts

- to plan the sentences of the final version of your answer

Training this way should help you to write short but clear answers. At the same time, you will be reviewing the major ideas for the Competency Test.

The other parts of the book, such as the review charts in the Appendix, should help you just before the Competency Test. At the end of the book there is a full practice Competency Test. You should try to take it as if it were the actual Competency Test. Work with your teacher on correcting it. There is also a set of "Last Minute Review Exercises." Use them to build your confidence just before the Competency Test. They should help you to remember the the main themes we've presented.

We wish you great success on the Competency Test.

The Authors

Assignments

Lesson	Readings	Pages	Questions	Date Due
1				
2				
3				
4				
5				
6				
7				
8				
9				
10				

LESSON 1

The Constitution:

Framework For American Government

The 13 colonies became "The United States of America" in 1776. Thomas Jefferson listed in the *Declaration of Independence* the reasons why the colonies broke away from Great Britain. The Declaration also included a general statement about democratic government. It said that all men are created equal. It also said, all men are given certain rights to life, liberty, and the pursuit of happiness. Finally, it said governments are created by the people and may be changed by the people. Yet, the Declaration *did not* create a new government. The Continental Congress knew the country needed a workable government if the country were to survive.

In 1781, the Continental Congress finally drew up a plan of government called the **Articles of Confederation**. It created a very weak central government. There was no chief executive or president. There was a **unicameral** (one house) legislature, but it had little power to tax or to raise an army. It lasted fewer than ten years (1781-89).

Under the Articles of Confederation, the states kept their **autonomy** (independent authority). This is understandable. The states were fighting for independence from Britain. They did not want to substitute one strong central authority for another.

The government under the Articles of Confederation had trouble handling the problems facing the new nation. Within a short time, many people wanted to rewrite the Articles or to change them completely.

In 1787, Congress called a Constitutional Convention in Philadelphia. The convention drafted a new document, the **United States Constitution**. It was not an easy task. The convention members agreed that the United States needed a stronger central government. They felt the people needed a chief executive (president) and a court system (judicial branch). They also felt Congress needed greater power to tax, to regulate commerce (trade), and to recruit an army.

Agreeing on how to meet these needs was difficult. There were many compromises. The major one, the **Great Compromise**, was concerned with the question of how to set up Congress. The states with large populations wished representation to be determined by population. The states with small populations wanted all states to be represented equally. Finally, the convention created a **bicameral** (two house) legislature. In the House of Representatives, population determines the number of seats a state receives. In the Senate, all states receive two seats.

After much debate and compromise, the states ratified the Constitution in 1789. This document still governs the United States today. It sets up a representative government (elected officials). It separates powers among three branches which check and balance each other. Also, it divides power between the national and state governments (federalism). The Constitution has lasted because it is very general and flexible. There are also many ways to change or amend it to meet new challenges.

Exercise 1:

Between 1776-1787, three great documents were very influential in forming the United States of America: the *Declaration of Independence*, the *Articles of Confederation*, and the *United States Constitution*. Match the ideas in Column A with the appropriate document from Column B.

Column A

A 1. written by Thomas Jefferson

+ **B** 2. first government of the U.S.

C 3. "bundle of compromises"

A 4. "all men are created equal"

+ **B** 5. contained a one-house legislature

+ **C** 6. bicameral legislature

+ **B** 7. governed the U.S.A. during its first years

C 8. Great Compromise

B 9. weak central government

+ **B** 10. government created 200 years ago

Column B

A. *Declaration of Independence*, 1776

B. *Articles of Confederation*, 1781-1789

C. *United States Constitution*, 1789 - present

Federalism: Relationship Between The National And State Governments

By revising the Articles of Confederation, the Philadelphia convention of 1787 sought to strengthen the confederation of states. In a **confederation**, the individual states keep most of their power or authority. If a central government needs to do only a few simple things, a confederation works well. For example, in the **Iroquois Confederacy** (also called the "Haudenosaunee Union") the individual tribes kept most of their power. A central council decided disputes. In the same sense, the **United Nations** also might be called a confederation. The U.N. suggests peaceful solutions to international problems, but it cannot force member nations to follow its suggestions.

The members of the Constitutional Convention of 1787 knew the country needed a central government with more authority. They eventually decided that a confederation was too weak for their needs. They replaced it with a **federal system.**

A **Federal system** divides power into two levels. Federalism in the United States today creates one **national** government and fifty **state** governments. The national government (also called the Federal Government or United States Government) has ultimate power over issues that concern the nation as a whole. The states have the authority to control local matters.

Four Types Of Powers Under The Constitution

1. **Delegated.** Article I of the Constitution lists most of the powers of the national government. We call these specific powers **delegated powers**. In theory, the Constitution limits the powers of national government to these powers.

2. **Implied.** Article I also has a phrase called the "**elastic clause**." It lets Congress enact laws that are "*necessary and proper*" to carry out its delegated powers. The elastic clause gives Congress a second type of power called **implied power**. This means Congress can stretch its delegated powers to meet new situations. The elastic clause made the Constitution flexible. (*See the next segment of this lesson for more on the elastic clause.*)

3. **Reserved.** **Reserved powers** are left to the states. Many citizens feared the Constitution made the national government too powerful. In response to this fear, ten amendments called the **Bill of Rights** were added in 1791. (*See Lesson 3*). In the Bill of Rights, Amendment 10 says that powers not given to the national government are **reserved** to the states.

4. **Concurrent.** **Concurrent power** is shared by both the national and state governments which must have some powers in order to exist. For example, both must have the power to tax to get the **revenue** (money) needed to operate.

U.S. Constitution limits power by dividing it between
the National and state governments.

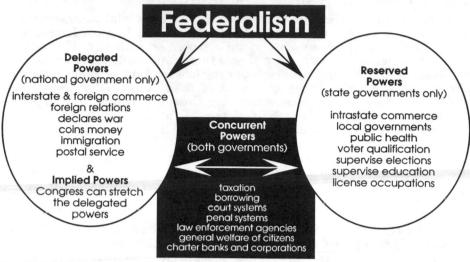

(Americans are citizens under two governments:
U.S. Federal Government and the state in which they reside.)

The Constitution is not perfectly clear on government power. Conflict over which level could make laws on slavery led to the **Civil War** (1861-65). Questions continue to arise over how far Congress can stretch the national government's power. Civil rights laws, the social security system, Hamilton's national bank, and the national 55 mph speed limit are other examples of the controversial use of the elastic clause by Congress.

The actions of U.S. Presidents and the Federal courts have also increased the power of the national government over the states. Federal Court decisions have overturned state laws on police investigations, abortion rights, and school desegregation.

Since the Civil War, the power of the national government has grown tremendously while state power has decreased. The industrialized nation needed more national laws when businesses, transportation, and communication systems crossed state lines.

New powers for the national government evolved during major reform periods of the 20th century: the *Progressive Era* 1900-1920; the *New Deal* 1933-1945; and the *Great Society* 1964-68. The national government began to act as the protector of the individual in conflicts with the state. We still debate these issues today. For example, deciding which level of government has the right to regulate abortion is very controversial.

The United States is not the only nation in the world with a federal system. Canada, Mexico, Germany, and Brazil also have federal systems. Canada's provinces are roughly the equivalent of our states.

Exercise 2:
Many key phrases describe the government of the United States created by the Constitution. Identify the term in each definition below.

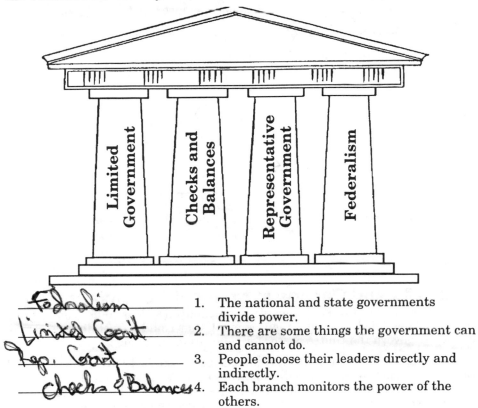

___Federalism___ 1. The national and state governments divide power.

___Limited Gov't___ 2. There are some things the government can and cannot do.

___Rep. Gov't___ 3. People choose their leaders directly and indirectly.

___Checks & Balances___ 4. Each branch monitors the power of the others.

Exercise 3:
Complete the sentences by filling in the blanks. Use the terms in the box on the following page.

1. Federalism is often defined as the ___division___ of powers between the ___State___ and the ___Federal___ governments.

2. The Constitution gives the national government the right to raise and to maintain an army and navy, to establish post offices, and to declare war. These are examples of ___delegated___ powers. The national government can stretch its authority by using the ___elastic___ clause. This gives the national government ___implied___ powers. The states have ___reserved___ powers to set guidelines for hunting and fishing licenses, traffic laws, marriage and drinking ages, and general education requirements.

3. Federalism has changed over the course of the last two hundred years. During the 20th Century, the Federal Government's power grew. This is a result of __Congress__ use of the elastic clause and federal __court__ rulings. __Industrialization__ created a need for more national laws. State power __declined__ as commerce developed on a nationwide scale.

4. Federalism exists in other government systems in the world. __Canada__ divides power among the national government, centered in Ottawa, and the governments of its various __Provinces__. In 1991, the federal system of the Union of Soviet Socialist Republics disintegrated. The fifteen former __republics__ are now fifteen separate nations.

Canada	delegated	implied	provinces
Congress	division	industrialization	republics
Court	elastic	national	reserved
declined			state

Flexibility And Change In National Government

The members of the 1787 Constitutional Convention could not see into the future. They tried to create a government that could peacefully and democratically govern the United States for generations to come.

How has the Constitution met challenges over the last two hundred years? Several sections in the original Constitution made it flexible. Some government actions have set **precedents** (acts that serve as guides in future cases). These precedents created procedures that allowed the Federal Government to survive many crises.

Government Change Through The Constitution

The Amendment Process	Allows new items to be added or parts of the original Constitution to be changed. Over the last two centuries, there have been only two dozen changes using the amendment process. The first ten were bundled together in 1791 as the **Bill of Rights**. Since then, Congress proposed numerous amendments, but few have been ratified by the necessary 3/4th majority of the states (see Constitution Summary in Appendices).
The Elastic Clause	Congress has the authority to stretch its delegated powers. With **implied power**, Congress creates laws which are "*necessary and proper*" to meet new situations. **Loose constructionists** support the use of this broad clause. **Strict constructionists** oppose its use. This power has caused some of the deepest controversies in our nation's history.

In the early years under the Constitution (1789-1825), government took actions that established new ways of doing things. These **precedents** set patterns that were followed when similar situations arose. These precedents make up "the unwritten constitution" because there is no direct mention of them in the original Constitution.

Government Change Through Precedents

- **The Cabinet**
  - George Washington gathered the heads of the executive departments into a group of close advisors to help him make decisions and solve problems. Presidents have had **cabinets** ever since. The Cabinet has been very influential under some presidents.

- **Political Parties**
  - Many of our early leaders felt **political parties** divided people when they needed to compromise. Still, a two party system gradually evolved. Each party tries to come up with ways to meet our problems and gain power in the government.

- **Judicial Review**
  - In the early 1800's, the Supreme Court assumed this power to declare federal laws and government actions to be unconstitutional (see *Marbury v. Madison*, 1803). Later, the Court expanded its power to review state laws and actions. Over the years, the use of judicial review has led to much defining and redefining of government power.

Exercise 4:

Use the two charts (above and opposite page) to classify the following government changes. Use a "C" if they are based on power clearly granted in the Constitution or a "P" if they are based on a precedent.

P 1. Supreme Court's declaring a law unconstitutional

C 2. George Washington's creating a Cabinet

C 3. Citizens guaranteed jury trials

P 4. Democrat's and Republican's becoming powerful groups

C 5. Federal Income Tax created

P 6. Voting rights for women established

P 7. Congress' creating the Air Force

P 8. Supreme Court's ordering schools to desegregate

Additional References On "The Constitution: Framework For American Government"

Check your textbook or N&N's *United States History and Government, A Competency Review Text* on:
- European, colonial, and Native American roots [pgs. 10-12]
- Federalists vs. anti-Federalists [pg. 17]
- Compromise at the Constitutional Convention [pg. 18]
- The Bill of Rights [pgs. 20-21]
- Structure of the U.S. Government [pgs. 23-33]
- List of specific amendments [pg. 329]
- Federalist controversies [pgs. 34-40]
- Supreme Court decisions under Chief Justice John Marshall [pg. 37]

Questions

1   The members of the 1787 Constitutional Convention created a government
   1   that officially broke away from Great Britain
   2   based upon a federal system
   3   that was very weak
   4   with no chief executive

2   The *Articles of Confederation* and the *United States Constitution* are similar because both
   1   established strong central governments
   2   governed the United States for hundreds of years
   3   provided frameworks for the United States Government
   4   created three co-equal branches

3   Which is a *concurrent* power of both the United States and New York State Governments?
   1   declare war on another nation
   2   collect income taxes
   3   tax imports
   4   establish immigration quotas

4   In the *Declaration of Independence*, Thomas Jefferson spoke of government by "consent of the governed." This means
   1   the people elect government officials
   2   powers are divided between the national and state governments
   3   there are three branches of government
   4   Congress can check the power of the President

5   Which statement is an opinion rather than a fact?
   1   The use of implied powers by Congress increased the power of the Federal Government.
   2   The Federal Government's power increased greatly in this century.
   3   The amendment process allowed the government to adapt to changing times.
   4   The Federal Government should decide on important matters such as abortion and civil rights.

6   Which deals directly with the flexibility of the Constitution?
1   dividing power between states and the Federal Government
2   limiting Congress to certain delegated powers
3   the amendment process
4   creation of the Supreme Court

Essay

Answer Part A on the lines provided. Use a separate sheet to do Part B.

For over 200 years, the United States of America based its government on several democratic ideas.

Democratic ideas
Federalism
Flexibility
Limited government
Representative government

Part A
Choose *two* of the democratic ideas from the list above. For *each*, 1) give a specific example of how that idea exists in U.S. Government, and 2) explain why this idea preserves democracy. [4]

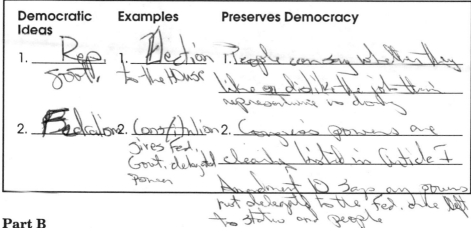

Democratic Ideas	Examples	Preserves Democracy
1. Rep. Govt.	1. Election to the House	1. People can say whether they like or did like the job their representative is doing
2. Federalism	2. Constitution gives Fed. Govt. delegated power	2. Congress powers are clearly listed in Article I. Amendment 10 says any powers not delegated to the Fed. are left to states and people

Part B
You should use Part A information in your Part B answer. However, you may include different or additional information in your Part B answer. [6]

Write an essay explaining why democratic ideas are the basis for United States Government.

LESSON 2

Separation Of Powers:
Three Branches Of Government

Great thinkers of the past influenced our Constitution. The European **Enlightenment** of the 17th and 18th Centuries had a powerful influence. For example, England's **John Locke** contributed the idea that government receives its power from the people it governs.

A French Enlightenment philosopher, **Baron de Montesquieu**, believed government should have **limited power**. He recommended dividing government powers among three branches. He said each branch should be assigned a specific job. Also, he thought each branch should control the others through a series of **checks and balances**.

The writers of the United States Constitution used the ideas of Locke and Montesquieu. The major role of **Congress** (legislative branch) is passing legislation. The major job of the **President** (executive branch) is enforcing laws and court decisions. The major role of the **Federal Courts** (judicial branch) is interpreting the law. Each branch has powers to check the other two branches. The chart below illustrates this.

Separation of Powers
Government Responsibilities

President	Congress	Judiciary
Vetoes Laws	Makes Laws Overrides Vetoes	Reviews Constitutionality of Laws
	Impeaches Allocates Funds	
Makes Treaties	Ratifies Treaties	Interprets Treaties
Makes Executive Appointments	Approves Executive Appointments	
Appoints Court Members	Creates Courts Approves Court Appointments	Reviews Executive Actions

We choose the people who serve in these branches in different ways. Congress (currently 435 Representatives and 100 Senators) is closest to the people. The public votes directly for the members of the House of Representatives. Originally, state legislatures appointed two United States Senators. The 17th Amendment now requires that Senators be directly elected by the people.

People do not choose officials in the other two branches directly. The people of each state choose "electors" who then decide who will be President and Vice-President. We call this the "electoral college." The President appoints judges of the Federal Courts, but they must be approved by the Senate.

Exercise 1:
Complete the blanks on the chart.

Branch	Name of Branch	Power	How are members selected today?
Legislative			
Executive			
Judicial			

The Federal Government has three branches, but they are not equal in power. At different points in our history, one branch has been more powerful than the others. Power depends on events and the personalities of the leaders. There has often been conflict among the branches.

Exerting Power: Strong Presidents
The office of President of the United States is a powerful position. As the role of the United States in the world increased, the power of the President increased. In times of national or world crises, the nation looks to the President for leadership. Some of our Presidents have exercised enormous power. At times, this brings the Executive into conflict with the other branches of government.

The Constitution lists some of the President's powers (see diagram on opposite page). Other powers, such as being leader of his/her political party, grew from custom and tradition.

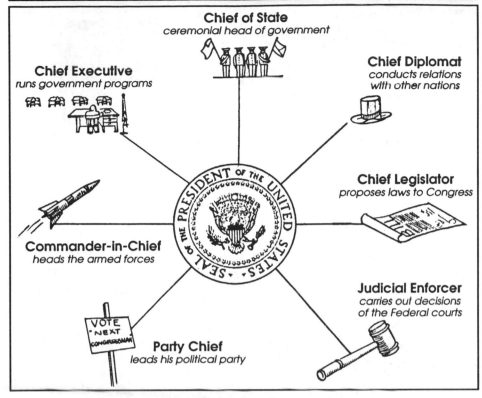

Chief of State
ceremonial head of government

Chief Executive
runs government programs

Chief Diplomat
*conducts relations
with other nations*

Chief Legislator
proposes laws to Congress

Commander-in-Chief
heads the armed forces

Judicial Enforcer
*carries out decisions
of the Federal courts*

Party Chief
leads his political party

Exercise 2:

Using the chart above, identify the role that the President is using.

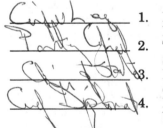

1. Roosevelt entertains the King and Queen of England at his home in Hyde Park, NY.
2. Truman has a summit meeting with Soviet leader Stalin in Germany.
3. Reagan suggests that Congress pass a major income tax cut for the people.
4. Bush sends U.S. troops to help defend Saudi Arabia against Iraq.

President Abraham Lincoln (1861-65) faced a major crisis – the Civil War. Lincoln took several questionable actions to help the Union win the war. When the war broke out, Congress was not in session. The President suspended the right to a **writ of habeas corpus** (he had people arrested without telling them the charges against them). Lincoln allotted money for the military without approval of Congress. Later, Congress approved many of Lincoln's unauthorized actions. Yet, the Supreme Court ruled his suspension of habeas corpus unconstitutional (*ex parte Milligan*, 1866).

President **Franklin D. Roosevelt** (1933-1945) had to deal with two crises - the Great Depression and World War II. When he won the 1932 election, the nation was in the midst of the Great Depression. Congress gave Roosevelt a free hand to deal with this crisis. He suggested a series of new laws and policies that became known as the **New Deal**.

Congress passed a number of New Deal actions. Generally, these laws increased the power of the national government to control the nation's economy. Critics argued many of these increases in power were unconstitutional.

The Supreme Court did rule some New Deal laws unconstitutional. To check the power of the Court, President Roosevelt wanted Congress to let him increase the number of justices. Congress checked Roosevelt by rejecting his "court packing scheme." Soon after, some elderly

Franklin D. Roosevelt

justices retired and FDR began appointing new men. The presidency of Franklin D. Roosevelt marked a huge growth in presidential power.

United States involvement in the Vietnam conflict increased tremendously during the administration of **President Lyndon B. Johnson** (1963-69). After an attack on an American naval ship, Congress passed the **Gulf of Tonkin Resolution**. This gave Johnson unlimited authority to fight the North Vietnamese.

Congress did not need to declare war formally. Military defense treaties, such as NATO and SEATO, already gave the president great power. Like Roosevelt, Johnson also persuaded Congress to pass a series of massive domestic programs. His **Great Society** programs aided cities, the environment, and the poor.

Lyndon B. Johnson

Under **President Richard Nixon** (1969-74), America ended military involvement in Vietnam. Congress passed laws (including the **War Powers Act** - 1973) to check the power of the President. Nixon tried to check Congress by vetoing it, but Congress overrode the veto (**veto**: the official rejection of legislation by the executive). This law is an attempt to check the President's power as Commander-in-Chief by restraining how he uses troops. As Chief Diplomat, Nixon set up a policy of **détente** (friendlier behavior) with the Soviet Union. He established better relations with Communist China.

While Nixon was strong in foreign affairs, some of his domestic actions led to his resignation. Congress investigated some questionable political and financial activities by President Nixon and his staff. The **Watergate Investigation** led Congress to consider impeaching Nixon (**impeach**: congressional power to accuse a president or a judge of misconduct in office). In the summer of 1974, before Congress completed the impeachment process, Nixon resigned. He became the first President to resign from office.

Richard M. Nixon

Exercise 3:

Complete the sentences by filling in the blanks. Use the terms in the box below.

Presidential power can be checked in several ways. Congress may

_____ *impeach* _____. The Supreme Court may rule a

presidential action or policy to be _*Watergate Invest.*_.

The power of the President of the United States often increases during

times of _*Pres. Lyndon*_ and _*Franklin Pres.*_ crisis.

Actions of Presidents Johnson and Nixon during the _*Great Society*_

led Congress to pass the _*New Deal*_.

> domestic
> international
> override a president's veto
> unconstitutional
> Vietnam Conflict
> War Powers Act

Checking Power: The Judicial Branch

The United States Constitution established one Supreme Court. The Constitution allowed Congress to create as many lower Federal courts as it wanted. The cases the Supreme Court hears deal with Constitutional issues. Its main power is **judicial review** (the ability to determine the constitutionality of governmental laws and actions). It can check Congressional laws and executive actions by declaring them to be **unconstitutional**. This power was not specifically mentioned in the Constitution. The Supreme Court took this power for itself in deciding the famous *Marbury v. Madison* (1803) case (see next page). Therefore, judicial review is part of the "unwritten constitution."

Some critics say that the Supreme Court exercises too much power for a non-elected body. They feel the Court violates Locke's principle of government by consent of the people. They believe that only elected officials, not appointed judges, should make major changes in public policy.

Examples Of The Checking Power
Of Supreme Court Decisions

Year	Case	Significance
1803	*Marbury v. Madison*	Supreme Court assumed the right of judicial review by declaring part of a 1789 judiciary act unconstitutional.
1819	*McCulloch v. Maryland*	Congress' use of the elastic clause to create a government bank was ruled constitutional.
1857	*Dred Scott v. Sandford*	Congressional compromise laws on slavery of 1820 and 1850 were ruled unconstitutional.
1866	*ex parte Milligan*	Even in war, the President cannot ignore **due process rights** of citizens accused of disloyal acts.
1936	*Butler v. United States*	Congress could not make laws regulating farmers' decisions. Part of the New Deal's Agricultural Adjustment Act was ruled unconstitutional.
1974	*Nixon v. United States*	Federal court ruling ordering the President to surrender executive files and tapes to Congress was ruled constitutional.

Exercise 4:

Complete the sentences by filling in the blanks. Use the terms in the box on the following page.

The Constitution divides the Federal Government into 3 branches. These

are the __ex_____ , _____ , and _____ branches.

If Congress passes a law and the President does not agree with it, he may

__veto_____ it. If Congress still wishes to pass it, they may __over_____

the President's __veto_____ . In 1973, during the Vietnam War, Congress

__over__ (ord)____ President Nixon's __veto____ and passed the War

Powers Act, which limits Presidential military power.

Congress may check the President in other ways. The Senate alone has

the authority to __ratify_____ treaties and __approve_____

presidential appointments. One treaty the Senate did not agree to was the

_____ which ended World War I. The entire Congress

votes on laws the President may suggest. If Federal Government money is to

be spent, Congress must __appropriate____ funds.

The Supreme Court may declare acts and laws of the government to be

_____ . We call this power to review these laws and

acts _____ _____ . Federal Court judges are

_____ by the _____ and approved by the

_____ . The Supreme Court struck down several of President

Franklin Roosevelt's _____ _____ programs. This

led to FDR's _____ _____ _____ to add more

justices. _____ rejected this attempt to change the Court.

approve	legislative	President
appointed	judicial	ratify
allocate or appropriate	judicial review	Senate
Congress	New Deal	Treaty of Versailles
court packing scheme	override	unconstitutional
executive	overrode	veto (*use 3x*)

Additional References On "Separation Of Power"

Check your textbook or N&N's *United States History and Government, A Competency Review Text* on:
- Andrew Johnson's impeachment [pg. 62]
- Rejection of the Treaty of Versailles [pgs. 161-163]
- FDR's Court Packing [pg. 194]
- Watergate [pgs. 293-294]

Questions

1   Checks and balances would be violated if Congress could
    1   declare a Presidential act unconstitutional
    2   vote to send money and troops to Saudi Arabia
    3   approve Supreme Court nominees
    4   impeach a President

2   An important job of the Supreme Court is
    1   enforcing the laws
    2   deciding what the Constitution means
    3   advising the President on foreign affairs
    4   advising the Congress on states' rights

3   Which constitutional power allowed the United States military to become involved in South Vietnam?
    1   Congress' ability to declare war
    2   Supreme Court's power of judicial review
    3   President's power as Commander-in-Chief
    4   Congress' power to veto laws

Base your answers to questions 4 and 5 on the cartoon below and on your knowledge of social studies.

4   Which idea is best illustrated by this cartoon?
1   judicial review
2   growth of executive power
3   impeachment
4   states' rights

5   During which time period might this cartoon have been published?
1   Industrial Revolution
2   Vietnam conflict
3   Cold War
4   New Deal

6   Which was the result of a Supreme Court decision?
1   Congress received Nixon's Watergate tapes
2   America sent troops to Vietnam
3   U.S. astronauts landed on the Moon.
4   U.S. declaration of war on Japan in 1941

Essay

The United States Constitution organizes a government of three branches: executive, legislative, and judicial. Each branch has the power to check *and* balance the others.

Part A

State *one* reason why the Constitution created a system of checks and balances. [1]

To keep all the powers in line

Identify *one* way the executive branch may check the legislative branch. [1]

Through vetos

Identify *one* way the legislative branch may check the executive branch. [1]

Through votes

Identify *one* way the judicial branch may check the other branches. [1]

Through congress

Part B

You should use Part A information in your Part B answer. However, you may include different or additional information in your Part B answer. [6]

Write an essay describing how the branches of the Federal Government keep power under control.

Protection Of Constitutional Rights And Liberties

Americans believe that their government exists for the people — to protect them and to preserve their freedoms. This belief goes back to our colonial roots. In the *Declaration of Independence* (1776), Thomas Jefferson repeated the political ideals of the Age of Enlightenment – that government exists to serve the people.

Partial List of Bill of Rights Guarantees

Freedoms: speech, press, peaceful assembly

Free exercise of religion

No unreasonable, unwarranted searches

No property taken without just compensation

Citizens accused of crimes will receive proper and equal legal procedures ["due process"]

Accused citizens will be informed of charges, get a speedy jury trial, be directly confronted by accusers at the trial, be able to call supportive witnesses

Accused citizens will not be forced to incriminate themselves

No excessive bail and cruel or unusual punishment

Note: Complete list of the Bill of Rights and the Constitutional Amendments is found in the Appendix on page 119.

Government should serve the people. But, history shows us thousands of examples of governments abusing their citizens, especially under absolute monarchs or totalitarian rule. In modern times, people try to protect themselves from tyranny, but daily news reports contain many stories of human rights violations in every part of the globe.

The Bill Of Rights

As we saw in Lessons 1 and 2, the writers of the Constitution strengthened the power of the Federal Government. They did not include very much protection for the individual citizen. Critics of the new Constitution feared that government could easily abuse citizens and ignore their civil liberties. The first Congress quickly developed the first ten amendments to the Constitution. They were ratified by the states in 1791. Today, we call them the Bill of Rights. They are still our main protection against tyranny.

The first ten amendments forbid Congress to take away personal freedoms. They also describe the defenses that individuals have when the government uses its power against them. Citizens should know their rights and fight to keep them. One role of the free public school system in the United States is to educate its citizens about rights and duties.

Because our Constitution and its amendments are so broad, questions are always arising. For example, we have a guarantee of freedom of speech. But, can a person say anything, to anyone, in any place, at any time? If you think the answer might be "no," you are correct. Freedom of speech sounds very clear but is really complex. Courts decide questions about our rights daily. Sometimes, Congress must pass laws to clarify issues. At other times, we have to amend the Constitution itself to make things clear.

Exercise 1:

List three ways rights already in the Bill of Rights can be made clear.

1. _Courts decide questions about our rights daily_
2. _Congress must pass laws to clarify issues_
3. _amendments to clarify the Constitution_

Expanding The Bill Of Rights

The Bill of Rights and other amendments guarantee our rights and civil liberties. But questions still arise about their exact meaning in different situations. The Supreme Court of the United States and lower Federal courts often have to clarify the meaning of our rights. For example, the courts have gradually ruled that the Federal Bill of Rights also protects individuals from abuses by state and local governments. The 14th Amendment is the basis for most of these rulings. It guarantees *"equal protection of the laws"* (equal justice) for all citizens.

The courts define and expand rights guaranteed in the Constitution. The table below contains some examples.

Supreme Court Decisions On Rights

Schenck v. United States (1919)	• The press is not completely free to publish anything it wants, especially if a "clear and present danger" to the security of the society exists.
Brown v. Bd. of Ed. of Topeka (1954)	• Racial segregation of schools violates the 14th Amendment's guarantee of equal justice. (See "Protection of Minority Rights" segment.)
Baker v. Carr (1962)	• The way some states set up election districts violated 14th Amendment's guarantee of equality ("one person-one vote").
Engle v. Vitale (1962)	• State rules requiring certain prayers be recited at the opening of the school day violated religious freedom.
Gideon v. Wainwright (1963)	• State laws denying legal counsel to accused citizens violated the 6th Amendment's "due process" clause.
Miranda v. Arizona (1966)	• Law enforcement authorities must tell citizens accused of crimes of their "due process" rights.

Exercise 2:

Match the statements in column 2 with the items in column 1.

_F_ 1. *Baker v. Carr*

_A_ 2. **Bill of Rights**

_C_ 3. *Brown v. Board of Ed.*

_H_ 4. *Declaration of Independence*

_J_ 5. public education

_D_ 6. *Engle v. Vitale*

_G_ 7. 14th Amendment

_K_ 8. *Gideon v. Wainwright*

_E_ 9. *Miranda v. Arizona*

_F_ 10. *Schenck v. United States*

_B_ 11. Supreme Court

A. protections against government abusing citizens

B. interprets rights

C. banned racial segregation in public education

D. state can not dictate religion

E. police must read accused persons their rights

F. limited publishing in time of national danger

G. guarantees all citizens equal justice

H. government serves the people

I. one person equals one vote

J. citizens learn rights and obligations

K. accused have the right to counsel (a lawyer)

Struggle For Equal Rights For Women

Today, we believe all citizens have the same basic constitutional rights. This has not always been the case. Women and minorities have had to struggle for equality.

In the European and Asian societies from which American settlers came, women traditionally played an inferior role to men.

In the 18th Century, when our government emerged, this was still true. The general protections of the Bill of Rights did not apply to women. They were not allowed to vote. Married women were under the legal authority of their husbands. Unmarried women were controlled by their fathers or another male relative.

In the 19th Century, powerful social forces such as public education, industrialization, and urbanization helped women begin a movement for equal rights. In 1848, at Seneca Falls, NY, the first women's rights convention issued the ***Declaration of Sentiments***. It became an important statement making society recognize its mistreatment of women. Even after the Civil War when slaves were freed, rights of women were denied.

In the Progressive Era, women achieved one of their goals, the right to vote. Their roles changed from "homemakers" into wage earners in the factories and offices of America. In 1920, victory came to the **suffragettes** (campaigners for womens' right to vote). Passage of the **19th Amendment** gave all American women the right to vote.

A new phase of the drive for the equality of women developed in the 1960's. Its goals were economic equality, including equal pay for equal work, and an **Equal Rights Amendment (ERA)** to the Constitution.

In 1961, a presidential committee on the status of women called for legal reforms. Most sexual discrimination before the law, in politics, and in business had to come to an end. This began a new phase in the Womens' Rights Movement (see the chart on the next page).

Modern Rights Of Women's Movement

• **Equal Pay Act** (1963)	• Men and women doing the same job should receive equal pay.
• **Title VII** of the **Civil Rights Act of 1964**	• Discrimination against women in employment and job promotions was prohibited.
• **National Organization of Women** (NOW)	• Founded in 1966, raised women's consciousness of their inferior status in American society. NOW pursues change through legislative and judicial channels. It spearheads campaigns for equal rights.
• **Higher Education Act** (1972)	• Discrimination against women in colleges was forbidden. (By 1980, all public, and most private colleges, were coeducational.)

In 1972, women's groups proposed an **Equal Rights Amendment** (ERA) to the Constitution. Its purpose was to guarantee equality with men in all circumstances. It said, *"Equality of rights under the law shall not be denied or abridged by the United States or any state on account of sex."* It won quick approval in Congress, but twice failed to gain the approval of the 3/4 of the states necessary to be a Constitutional Amendment.

Statistics show that women earn considerably less than men. Women's rights groups claim that much of the inequality comes from the fact that women are paid less than men even when jobs are similar in nature. Some states have passed **comparable worth** (*equal-pay-for-equal-work*) laws that order the same pay scale for jobs requiring similar skills. Womens' groups want more publicly funded day-care facilities for children. Many mothers wish to continue careers while raising a family.

Help Wanted

Cleaning Woman
$5 per hour

Sanitary Engineer
$10 per hour

Women have made tremendous advances in the workplace. Many still find roadblocks when seeking positions in management. This is especially true for women assuming jobs traditionally held by males. Some firms have used government inspired **affirmative action programs** (hiring more women and minorities to create a justly balanced workforce). Cries of "reverse discrimination" have made these programs controversial.

Exercise 3:

Use the clues at the bottom to fill in the missing words.

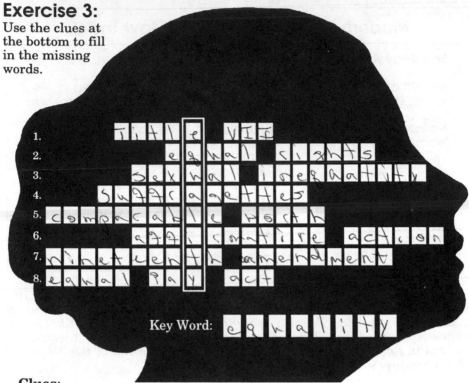

1. Title VII
2. equal rights
3. sexual inequality
4. suffragettes
5. comparable worth
6. affirmative action
7. nineteenth amendment
8. equal pay act

Key Word: equality

Clues:
1. forbade sex discrimination in the workplace
2. states failed to ratify this amendment
3. major job problem today
4. Progressive Era campaigners for right to vote
5. state "equal-pay-for-equal-work" laws
6. hiring preference to women and minorities
7. gave American women the right to vote
8. men and women doing the same job should receive the same pay

Struggles For Minority Rights

Minority groups, such as African Americans, Hispanic, and Native Americans, are often denied basic rights and equal justice. After the Civil War, the **13th, 14th,** and **15th Amendments** freed former slaves, made them equal citizens, and ensured their right to vote (suffrage). Later, when Reconstruction ended in the 1870's, Southern state leaders found ways to get around these amendments. **"Jim Crow Laws"** created **de jure** (legalized) **segregation** throughout the South.

Civil rights groups challenged Southern racial separation. In 1896, the U.S. Supreme Court in *Plessy v. Ferguson* upheld segregation. The Court said it was fair if equal facilities were provided for both races. As a result, Jim Crow laws segregated transportation, education, dining, and entertainment facilities throughout the South.

In the 20th Century, African American leaders campaigned against Jim Crow laws in the South. White segregationists easily blocked any political attempts to challenge their power. After World War II, the Truman and Eisenhower administrations tried to use Federal power to end racial segregation. But, Southern leaders in Congress checked these efforts.

A breakthrough came in 1954. The Supreme Court issued its monumental decision in ***Brown . v. the Board of Education of Topeka***. The Court applied the 14th Amendment's *"equal protection of the laws"* clause against various state segregation laws. It announced that racial segregation of schools violated that part of the Constitution. The Court ordered racial segregation to end.

The decision outraged Southern leaders. They claimed that education was a state matter. They said the Supreme Court had no jurisdiction over it. In some states, militia and state police kept African Americans from registering.

Angry mobs threatened violence. In 1957, the Governor of Arkansas refused to obey a Federal court order to admit African American students to Little Rock Central High School. President Eisenhower would not allow such a public challenge to the Constitution. He sent regular U.S. Army troops to escort the students into the school.

Also in 1957, the Civil Rights Movement gained power. Under leaders such as Dr. Martin Luther King, Jr., the movement challenged Congress to overcome the Southern opposition. Congress passed acts to defeat discrimination against minorities. The chart below lists some of these actions:

**Dr. Martin
Luther King Jr.**

Actions For Minority Rights	
Act	**Result**
Civil Rights Act of 1957	• created a Civil Rights Commission to investigate injustices; authorized the Department of Justice to ensure voting rights for African Americans in the south
Civil Rights Act of 1960	• furthered voting rights
Civil Rights Act of 1964	• forbade discrimination in all federally funded activities, set up an Equal Opportunity Commission to end job discrimination
24th Amendment (1964)	• forbade use of poll taxes in Federal elections (can't be denied vote because of lack of funds)
Voting Rights Act of 1965	• ended most legal blocks to voter registration in the south
Civil Rights Act of 1968	• forbade discrimination in housing and strengthened penalties for job discrimination

Exercise 4:

Sort the items below on the basis of whether they helped or hindered minorities in gaining basic rights.

> *Plessy v. Ferguson*
> *Brown v. the Board of Education of Topeka*
> Jim Crow Laws
> 13th, 14th, and 15th Amendments
> Civil Rights Acts (1957, 1960, 1964, and 1968)
> 24th Amendment
> Voting Rights Act of 1965

Helped Minorities to Gain Rights	Hindered Minorities from Gaining Rights

Additional References On "Constitutional Rights"

Check your textbook or N&N's *United States History and Government, A Competency Review Text* on:
- Civil rights protests [pg. 258]
- Expansion of suffrage: women, African Americans [pgs. 130, 257, 273]
- Treatment of the American Indian [pgs. 277]
- Individual rights in wartime [pgs. 160, 217]

Questions

1   Protection of individual rights was the main purpose of
   1   the original Constitution of 1787
   2   the first ten amendments to the Constitution
   3   state and local laws
   4   actions by the President

2   According to the *Declaration of Independence*,
   1   people cannot question their government
   2   women and minorities have fewer rights than other citizens
   3   government serves the people
   4   discrimination is unconstitutional

3   Which has *most frequently* broadened the meaning of the Bill of Rights?
1   local governments
2   Presidential actions
3   the needs of the nation during war
4   decisions of the Supreme Court

4   "Due process" assures citizens accused of crimes will have
1   freedom of speech
2   the right to bear arms
3   no property taken without just compensation
4   proper and equal legal procedures

5   The primary goal in the struggle for womens' rights in the 19th and early 20th Centuries focused on
1   equal pay for equal work
2   job promotions
3   voting rights
4   better housing

6   In *Plessy v. Ferguson* (1896), the Supreme Court upheld
1   slavery
2   racial segregation
3   equality for African Americans
4   voting rights for women

7   On which constitutional principle was *Brown v. Bd. of Ed. of Topeka* (1954) based?
1   federalism
2   equal protection of the law
3   checks and balances
4   representative government

Base your answer to questions 8 and 9 on the graph at the right and on your knowledge of social studies

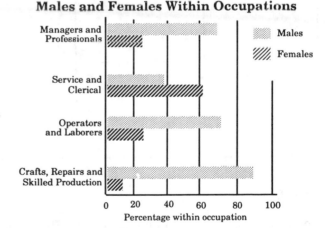

Males and Females Within Occupations

8   Today, women make up 50% of the workforce of the U.S. Which occupation category on the graph best reflects this?
1   managers and professionals
2   service and clerical
3   operators and laborers
4   crafts, repairs, and skilled production

9   Which factor has caused the general pattern shown in the graph?
1   a rise in the number of senior citizens
2   a general decline in the nation's birth rate
3   an increase in the number of women eligible to vote
4   inequality in hiring practices

Essay

Different methods have been used to make sure that all citizens of the United States have equality.

Methods
Affirmative action programs
Supreme Court decisions
Constitutional Amendments
Acts of Congress

Part A

Choose *two* methods from the list above. For *each* method,

1) give a specific example of what method is being used to gain equality, and
2) explain how the method succeeded. [4]

Method	Examples	Success of Method
1. _____ _____	1. _____ _____	1. _____ _____ _____ _____
2. _____ _____	2. _____ _____	2. _____ _____ _____ _____

Part B

You should use Part A information in your Part B answer. However, you may include different or additional information in your Part B answer. [6]

Write an essay explaining how different methods have been used successfully to make sure that all citizens of the United States have equality.

L E S S O N 4

Citizen Participation And Responsibility

In a democracy, the people make important political decisions. Life is too complex for citizens to vote on every issue facing every level of government. Because of this, the United States is an indirect democracy, or **republic**. In a republic, the people choose **representatives** who make most of the government decisions.

In our republic, we vote for representatives to school and town boards, village and city councils, county and state legislatures, and the United States Congress. We also have to vote for administrators at all levels, from city mayors and town supervisors to the President of the United States.

To make democracy work, voting is not enough. We must accept the responsibility for monitoring the activities of our elected officials. We must make them aware of our feelings on issues.

There are so many levels of government and so many issues at each level that it is easy for us to feel overwhelmed. Some of us shrug off our responsibility. We become **apathetic** (not caring). When citizens of a democracy become apathetic, corruption or tyranny results.

An alternative to being apathetic is to join groups to monitor officials. Political groups take different forms. One type of group is a **lobby** (special interest group). Lobbies watch and respond to government officials' actions on specific issues. Examples of lobbies include: Consumers Union (consumer protection), the National Rifle Association (gun control), the American Federation of Labor (labor laws), and the American Medical Association (laws affecting the medical profession).

Another type of political group is a **political party**. It represents citizens' feelings on a wide range of major issues. Parties also nominate candidates who reflect party feelings to run for elected offices. The two major parties in the United States evolved in the 19th Century. The Democrats and Republicans sometimes agree on *what* government should do, but disagree on *how* it should be done. The two major parties are often so close on issues, that **third parties** emerge at different times to represent those who want different solutions to political problems. (See section on third parties on page 40.)

Most Americans cherish freedom. At home, in school, and from the media, they learn that freedom rests on steady participation to keep democracy alive.

Exercise 1:

If democracy is to continue, each generation must accept the responsibility

for ___electing___ and ___monitoring___ officials. A primary

function of the political party is to ___nominate___ candidates.

Citizen Participation: Voting

Although we assume all American citizens have the right to vote, universal suffrage did not exist in the early years of our country. Many groups, such as women and minorities, struggled to win voting rights (see Lesson 3).

When the nation began, state laws limited **suffrage** (voting rights) to the older, literate, property owning white males. Americans' ideas about equality changed, and, one by one, state laws, Congressional laws, and Constitutional amendments changed these voting requirements.

Constitutional Expansion Of Voting Rights

Amendment	Result
15th Amendment (1870)	• clarifies all citizens' rights to vote and forbids denial of voting rights because of race
19th Amendment (1920)	• forbids denial of voting rights because of sex (women's suffrage)
23rd Amendment (1961)	• grants citizens of Washington D.C. the right to vote in presidential elections
24th Amendment (1964)	• forbids the use of poll taxes in Federal elections
26th Amendment (1971)	• voting age set at 18 in all states

Citizen Participation:
Political Parties

In a democracy, the power to get things done rests in majority rule. In a republic, this means choosing a majority of representatives who will do things the way you want. People must join forces with like-minded people and convince others to elect their favorite candidates.

From the start of United States history, people formed political parties. The two party system began with the **Federalist** and the **Democratic-Republican** parties of the 1790's. Today we have the Republicans and Democrats. These national parties are very loosely organized, with most of the leadership at state levels. They hold **primary elections** and **conventions** among their members to select candidates. They raise money and organize campaigns to influence voters' choices.

Today, only about one-third of American voters register in political parties. The members of political parties are the people who pick the candidates who appear on the ballots on election day. Therefore, active party members on state, county, and local levels are very powerful and influential.

A citizen who wishes to run successfully for office has to convince party leaders he or she would be a good candidate. He or she must get leaders' support in **primaries** (elections to choose candidates) and **conventions** (meetings to choose candidates). Once the party chooses its candidate, it supplies campaign workers and money to campaign for election.

Beyond elections, political parties pressure successful candidates to follow the party's ideas once they're in office. Within legislative bodies such as Congress or the New York State Legislature, the Democrats and Republicans organize, pick leaders, and try to coordinate voting.

Citizen Participation: Third Parties

It is an important part of our heritage of freedom that people can speak out and organize politically. At different times in our history, groups of citizens have formed third parties to promote ideas held by minorities. This occurs because the two major parties fail to respond to the needs or ideas of all the citizens. There have been parties to oppose slavery, immigration, wars, alcoholic beverages, civil rights for African Americans, and abortion. Third parties have promoted the welfare of certain groups such as taxpayers, farmers, and industrial workers. There have also been third parties for radical change through fascism and communism.

The candidates of these third parties rarely win elections. They sometimes have strong regional appeal. A strong showing by a third party sometimes draws the attention of the major parties, which then adopt the cause or idea. This occurred with the progressive ideas of the Populists in the 1890's (see Lesson 6) and the Peace and Freedom Party's influence in the anti-Vietnam War movement of the late 1960's.

Exercise 2:

Match the phrases in column 2 with the ideas in column 1.

column 1:

H 1. suffrage
J 2. third parties
F 3. 15th Amendment
D 4. Federalist
I 5. 19th Amendment
E 6. primary elections
A 7. 24th Amendment
G 8. conventions
C 9. 26th Amendment
B 10. party help for candidates

column 2:

A. no poll taxes
B. campaign workers and financial resources
C. minimum voting age equals 18 years
D. early political party
E. in-party election to choose candidates
F. no race discrimination in voting
G. party meeting to choose candidates
H. the right to vote
I. no sex discrimination in voting
J. voice for minority

Citizen Responsibility:
Paying Taxes

In a democracy, citizens have certain duties such as serving in the armed forces and serving on juries to ensure justice. Citizens are also required to pay taxes. Taxes produce the **revenue** (money) to provide the services people need from governments.   These services include: national defense, public education, highway maintenance, income and health assistance for the disabled, elderly, and poor. Of course, there are always debates over the value of various government programs.

In the early stage of our nation's development, taxes were not as burdensome as they are today. We were a small, agrarian (farming) country, and governments at all levels had less to do. On the national level, the revenue came from three sources: **tariffs** (taxes on imported goods), **excises** (luxury taxes), and the sale of western lands. These revenues paid for a small army, the postal service, and the courts. The scope of the national government was not very wide. Most of the time, it had a **budget surplus** (it collected more money than it needed). On the state and local level, **property taxes** on real estate generated most of the revenue needed to take care of small primary schools and a few roads.

As the nation industrialized, the tasks of government mounted. Spending grew dramatically. Most Federally-owned land was sold to homesteaders. Tariffs and excises did not produce enough revenue. The Constitution was amended to create a Federal **income tax** (16th Amendment, 1913). It is a **progressive tax**. This means the income tax rate is based on the amount of income a person makes. For example, a person with a $10,000 annual income might pay 15%, while a person with a $100,000 income might pay 31%.

Exercise 3:

After reading all of this section on the Citizen Responsibility to Pay Taxes, create a caption for this cartoon.

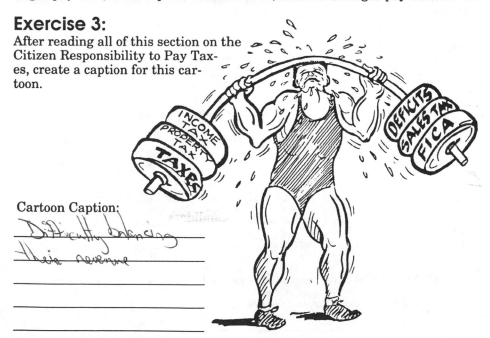

Cartoon Caption:

Difficulty balancing

their revenue

Today, the Federal Government spends a trillion dollars a year (an average of $7,000 per person). Personal and corporate income taxes generate most of the Federal revenue. **Social Security taxes** (FICA) makes up 35 percent. New York and many other states (and some localities) also have income taxes in addition to property taxes and sales taxes.

When you add the different forms of local, state, and Federal taxes together, an average family pays more than one-third of its annual income in taxes. Still, the U.S. ranks lower than most the top industrial countries in the amount of taxes citizens pay.

While the amount of money raised is huge, governments on most levels have **budget deficits**. This means governments cannot raise enough revenue to meet their financial obligations. They borrow heavily and sell bonds. Therefore, a large proportion of the money governments get from taxpayers is used for **interest payments** to lenders. About 15 cents of every tax dollar goes to pay interest on money the Federal Government borrowed and spent years ago. The total national debt accumulated over the past 20 years is more than two trillion dollars.

There are only two ways to reduce these debts: spend less (cut down government activities) or raise taxes (get more revenue). Neither action is popular.

Officials on all levels are under constant pressure to cut government expenses. Relaxation of Cold War tensions allows some Federal spending reductions for defense, but cutting welfare and other human services has proven nearly impossible. In 1985, Congress passed the **Gramm-Rudman-Hollings Act** to install mandated budget limits. So far, the limits have never been met.

Exercise 4:

Modified True or False: Correct false items by writing a different phrase for the *italicized* words.

F   1.   The average American family spends *10 percent* of its annual income on various kinds of taxes. 1/3 _____

_____

F   2.   Today, the chief sources of revenue for the Federal Government are *tariffs and excise taxes.* income taxes, selling bonds _____

T   3.   Today, the chief sources of revenue for states are *property taxes, income taxes, and sales taxes.* _____

_____

_____ 4. Large budget deficits have added a new expense category to government budgets: *interest payments*. _____

_____

_____ 5. Governments on most levels have *budget surpluses* because they cannot raise enough revenue to meet their financial obligations. __

Budget deficits _____

Additional References On "Citizen Participation And Responsibility"

Check your textbook or *N&N's United States History and Government, A Competency Review Text* on:
- Political Parties [pg. 36]
- Growth of Democracy [pgs. 14-47]
- Third Parties: Populist Party [pg. 121]
- Progressive Parties [pg. 141, 219]
- States' Rights Party [pg. 219]
- George Wallace [pg. 286]
- 1968 Democratic Convention [pg. 284]
- Federal budget deficit [pg. 305]

Questions

1   The United States Government is a(n)
   1   direct democracy
   2   dictatorship
   3   absolute monarchy
   4   republic

2   Political parties choose candidates for elected office through
   1   primary elections and conventions
   2   general elections
   3   Congressional legislation
   4   decisions of the Supreme Court

3   In the United States, third parties have
   1   often won a majority in Congress
   2   allowed political minorities to express themselves
   3   tried to overthrow the government
   4   no legal status

4   Both the United States Government and New York State Government raise revenue through
   1   sales taxes   3   income taxes
   2   tariffs   4   property taxes

5   Which of the following groups do the daily political decision-making in
     a republic?
     1   all of the citizens
     2   elected representatives and administrators
     3   appointed officials
     4   third party candidates

Base your answer to questions 6 and 7 on the graph below and on your
knowledge of social studies.

Average Taxes in Industrial Countries

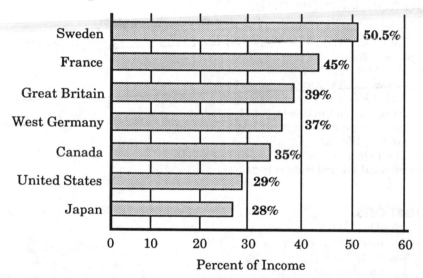

Percent of Income

6   The average tax rate for the nations shown is
     1   lowest in European nations
     2   nearly 40% of a person's income
     3   more than in underdeveloped countries
     4   a cause of deficit spending

7   According to the graph, taxpayers in the United States pay
     1   the highest taxes among the major industrial countries
     2   less than taxpayers in most industrial countries
     3   more than taxpayers in most industrial countries
     4   less than taxpayers in Japan

Essay

Democratic governments succeed only when citizens participate in political activities.

Political Activities

Voting
Paying taxes
Joining political parties
Serving jury duty

Part A

Choose *two* political activities from the list above. For each activity, list two ways the activity promotes democracy. [4]

Activity	Promotes Democracy
1. _____	1. _____
	_____
2. _____	2. _____
	_____

Part B

You should use Part A information in your Part B answer. However, you may include different or additional information in your Part B answer. [6]

Write an essay explaining why United States citizens must participate to keep democratic government alive.

LESSON 5

Industrial And Technological Growth

At the end of the 19th Century, business and industry in the United States grew tremendously. Inventions such as those of Thomas A. Edison allowed new machinery and businesses to develop. More goods were produced and transported to wider areas.

The number and size of corporations grew. Business leaders created new methods to protect themselves from economic recessions and depressions. They formed **monopolies**, **trusts**, and **pools** to protect their businesses.

Monopolies occur when a single firm has total control of the production and distribution of a product or service. **Andrew Carnegie** owned most of the iron mines, coal mines, steel mills, ships, and railroads manufactured and transported his steel.

Other monopolies tried to control other businesses producing the same goods. For this reason, **John D. Rockefeller** formed the Standard Oil Company of New Jersey. Unlike Rockefeller and Carnegie, **J. P. Morgan** did not build a single company. He created trusts by controlling enough stock to merge his companies into monopolies.

John D. Rockefeller

Andrew Carnegie

J. P. Morgan

The Federal Government had a **laissez-faire** (minimized regulation) economic policy. It avoided regulating business during this time. Today, Federal anti-trust acts preserve competition. The kind of power Carnegie, Rockefeller, and Morgan had is now illegal.

Industrial growth led to many other changes in the United States. The country became urbanized. Cities grew larger and served as the centers of commerce. Millions of immigrants, mostly from Europe, came to the United States seeking a better life. They provided the labor force needed in the industrial cities.

Not all people were happy with these changes. Some wanted Federal Government policies to limit the number and kinds of immigrants. Many demanded Federal Government economic policies to control the abuses and corruption of big business. Demands for reform and business growth continued into the 1900's.

Immigration And Urbanization

In the late 19th Century, the population of the United States increased dramatically. Thousands of immigrants came annually. Most came from Europe. The demand for workers was so high that many industries and states advertised in Europe for workers and settlers. In the late 19th Century, many immigrants were peasants who came from Southern and Eastern Europe. They left high land rents and taxes, poor soil, and religious conflict in their old countries. These Italians, Greeks, Slavs, Russians, Poles, and others dreamed of rich farmland in the American Midwest. Their poverty and lack of modern farm technology forced them to find work in the cities. They provided the muscle for the industrial era.

Northeastern cities, such as Boston, New York, Buffalo, Philadelphia, and Pittsburgh, had huge immigrant populations. Immigrants found work in the factories and provided the cheap labor America needed. They arrived with little or no money and settled into poorer neighborhoods. There they formed ethnic communities or **ghettos** (Little Italys, Chinatowns).

The cities offered the best and worst that industrialized America had to offer. Cities had libraries, museums, theaters, and vast public school and transportation systems. But rapid urban growth created problems. Industrial cities had poor sanitation, inadequate sewage systems, and foul water. Overcrowded living conditions made cities unhealthy.

Rapid growth also produced social conflict. Prejudice developed as immigrants poured into the country. America was predominantly a Protestant country. Most of the new immigrants from Southern and Eastern Europe were Catholic or Jewish.

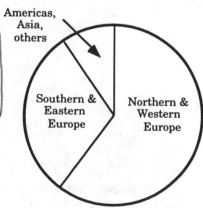

**Immigrant Origins
1880-1900**

"The cities offered the best and worst that industrialized America had to offer."

Religious and cultural differences led to hostility. Public reaction finally led Congress to pass laws limiting certain groups. Congress passed the Chinese Exclusion Act in 1882.

There were also economic problems. Desperate for survival, immigrants worked long hours for low wages. When the economy went into recessions and depressions, native born Americans blamed new immigrants for taking jobs and keeping wages low. This led to **nativist** (anti-immigrant) reactions. Nativist groups, such as the **American Protective Association**, called for a severe limit on immigration to the United States.

Later, the **Ku Klux Klan** pressured Congress to pass the first comprehensive immigration acts. In the 1920's, these acts established prejudicial **quotas** for each country and later abolished all immigration from Asia.

Despite the opposition, many immigrants adapted quickly to their new homeland. In the United States, immigrant contributions in the fields of science, politics, and the arts are many.

Today, new immigration policies have replaced the national origins system of the 1920's. These new policies set a general limit for each hemisphere. They also gave special consideration to those with relatives already in the United States. Job skills are also a factor in choosing immigrants. In addition, the United States admits large numbers of political refugees.

Most immigrants still settle in cities and work long hours for low pay. Today, immigrants come from Latin America and Asia. Many of today's immigrants are skilled professionals. Like all immigrants to the United States, they still seek a better life for themselves and their families.

**Immigration To
The United States**

Asia 35%

Europe 18%

Other 7%

Latin America 40%

1971 - 1980

Exercise 1:

List three reasons why most immigrants at the turn of the century settled in the cities of the United States.

1. _____

_____

2. _____

_____

3. _____

_____

Identify two major differences between the immigrants to the United States of one hundred years ago and those of today.

1. _____

_____

2. _____

_____

Why do people immigrate to the United States? _____

_____

_____

Reaction To Industrialization

In the late 1800's, people began to protest the business practices of the industrialists. Factory workers, farmers, and social reformers took action in different ways.

Factory workers put in long, hard hours and endured dangerous and unhealthy conditions. The workers and factory owners seldom knew each other directly. Owners hired managers to run the factories and make day-to-day decisions.

Workers began organizing **labor unions**. Unions wanted to negotiate with the bosses. They wanted **collective bargaining** for higher wages and better working conditions.

Unions organized two ways. **Craft unions** organized workers by their special skill (plumbers, electricians, carpenters). The **American Federation of Labor** (AF of L) united the major craft unions in the 1880's. Industrial unions organized workers within a particular industry. The **Congress of Industrial Organizations** (CIO) united the major industrial unions in the 1930's. In the 1950's these two organizations merged and formed the **AFL-CIO**. It is the largest single group of unions in the United States today.

Most owners and their managers did not want to bargain with unions. They claimed that such groups interfered with their right to run their businesses. Frustrated workers and employers often clashed violently.

The **strike** became the major weapon unions used to demand change. Strikes were frequent during the industrial era. Some succeeded, but most often they failed. Violent strikes caused the public to fear and distrust unions. The failure of the **Homestead Steel Strike** in 1892 removed unions from the steel industry until the 1930's.

While unionization helped workers deal with the abusive industrial system, farmers also fought back. The railroads were their biggest enemy. They charged very high rates to get the farmers' produce to market. From 1875-1900, many state legislatures passed laws to limit the power of the railroads.

The railroads challenged these laws. Supreme Court decisions of the era said that the states only had the right to regulate railroads within their boundaries (*Munn v. Illinois*, 1876). To control railroads nationally, Congress passed the **Interstate Commerce Act** in 1887. Other **anti-trust legislation** tried to control the power of monopolies. These early laws were weak but did start government's increasing control of big business.

The farmers also formed organizations such as **The Grange** to fight big business. Since business controlled the Democratic and Republican parties, some farmers formed new political parties. The most influential was the **Populist Party** of 1892. The Populists' platform included: government control of the railroads, graduated income tax, direct election of U.S. Senators, an eight hour work day, restrictions on immigration, and free coinage of silver. The Populists believed these policies would benefit the entire country. The Populists won few elections but did influence the major political parties. Congress eventually enacted many of their policies.

Exercise 2:

How did the farmers and the workers try to control the abuses of big business? Came up w/ political parties – strikes (Unions) govt laws

By the late 1800's and early 1900's, the American public was also calling for more Federal Government control of big business. Americans saw corruption in all levels of government. They felt the ruthless tactics of big business were ruining the free market. The industrial era created vast amounts of wealth for the owners of big business, but the era also left many in poverty. The gap between rich and poor was increasing while opportunity seemed to be decreasing.

A general movement for change arose in America. Well-educated middle class reformers became the center of the **Progressive Movement**. They centered attention on the conditions in the cities. In newspaper articles and magazines, writers exposed the corruption of city governments dominated by big business. Progressives called for women's suffrage, reform in all levels of government, greater control of big business, the prohibition of alcohol, and a Federal income tax.

Progressives came from both major political parties. Presidents Theodore Roosevelt, a Republican, and Woodrow Wilson, a Democrat, both had progressive viewpoints. Congress passed many laws to improve the quality of the American way of life. Four Constitutional amendments were ratified from 1913-1920: income tax, direct election of U.S. Senators, women's right to vote, and Prohibition. The Progressive movement declined as the United States became involved overseas during World War I.

Exercise 3:

Use the clues on the opposite page to fill in the missing words.

1. **I** NCOME tax
2.   some **N**
3. Builder **D**
4.   IND **U** STRIAL
5. Progre **S** sives
6.   **T** HIRD
7.   **R** eform
8. Collective **I**
9.   **A** FL
10.   Oil **L**
11.   Strike **I**
12. Unioni **Z** ation
13.   cr **A** ft
14. Populis **T**
15.   C **I** O
16. H **O** MESTEAD
17.   **N** ativist

Clues:

1. Progressive Era amendment
2. granted the right to vote during the Progressive era
3. caused farmers problems
4. broad unions that took in all workers in the company
5. reformers of the early 1900's
6. The Populists were a _____ party
7. to change for the better
8. union and management contract talks: _____ bargaining
9. organization composed of craft unions
10. Rockefeller's monopoly
11. powerful union action
12. process of labor organizing
13. skilled union
14. party that represented farm interests
15. organization of industrial unions formed in the 1930's
16. strike that removed unions from the steel industry for 40 years
17. anti-immigrant groups

Additional References On "Industrial Growth"

Check your textbook or N&N's *United States History and Government, A Competency Review Text* on:

- Southern industrialization [pgs. 67-68]
- Corruption in the Industrial Era [pg. 71]
- Industry before the Civil War [pgs. 79-80]
- Growth of the Railroads [pgs. 83-84]
- Carnegie, Rockefeller, and Ford [pgs. 86-88]
- Laissez-faire policy [pg. 89]
- Monopolies and trusts [pgs. 90-91]
- Nativist reaction to immigrants [pg. 111]
- Theodore Roosevelt and Woodrow Wilson [pgs. 138-143]

Questions

1   Some criticized the actions of business leaders such as Andrew Carnegie and John D. Rockefeller because they
    1   decreased American trade overseas
    2   donated vast amounts of money to the public
    3   allowed foreign factories to produce more than American ones
    4   eliminated competition

2   During the early stages of industrialization, the Federal Government's economic policy of laissez-faire led to
    1   businesses losing tremendous amounts of money
    2   Congress restricting immigration
    3   the development of large labor unions
    4   monopolies, pools, and trusts

Base your answer to question 3 on the graphs below and on your knowledge of social studies.

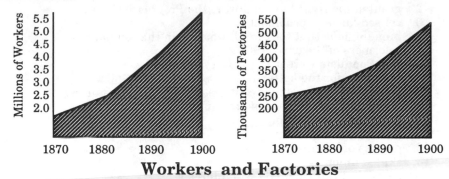

Workers and Factories

3   Which statement about the relationship between the number of factories and the number of workers from 1870-1900 is correct?
   1   The demand for factory workers increased.
   2   The size of the factories decreased.
   3   Each factory employed fewer and fewer workers.
   4   The factories moved to the suburbs during this time period.

Base your answer to question 4 on the cartoon below and on your knowledge of social studies.

4   The political cartoon above represented the views of some people during the industrial growth period of John D. Rockefeller, Andrew Carnegie, and J. P. Morgan. Which statement best represents the main idea of the cartoon?
   1   The laissez-faire economic policy of the Federal Government had little public support.
   2   The formation of monopolies, trusts, and pools are limited by government.
   3   Business feared government industrial controls.
   4   Big business had power over government.

5   The rise of big business, industrialization, and immigration added to
  1   the decline in the number of railroads
  2   an increase in the number of farms in the United States
  3   the growth of cities
  4   a decrease in the urban population

6   Reform groups such as the Populists and the Progressives called for
  1   a violent overthrow of private business by the workers
  2   major limits on the power of the labor unions
  3   a nation based on small farmers
  4   government to control the abuses of big business

7   One group in the United States that wanted to limit the number of
     immigrants was the
  1   factories owners
  2   labor union leaders
  3   slave holders
  4   railroad companies

Essay

Certain symbols remind us of how powerful a period of history can be.

Part A:

Select *three* of the symbols above and explain 1) how the symbol reflects change in the Age of Industrialization, and 2) whether the change was helpful to the country or not. [4]

Symbol	Change	How Helpful or Not?
1._____	1._____	1._____
	_____	_____
		_____
2._____	2._____	2._____
	_____	_____
		_____
3._____	3._____	3._____
	_____	_____
		_____

Part B:

You should use Part A information in your Part B answer. However, you may include different or additional information in your Part B answer. [6]

Write an essay discussing how changes to the United States during the Era of Industrialization influenced life in the United States.

LESSON 6

Economic Policies Of The United States Government

From its earliest years, the United States has been a **market economy**. In a market, consumers and producers want the freedom to make decisions in their best interests.

Adam Smith described the great benefits of such economic freedom in *The Wealth of Nations* (1776). He said a free market economy works best with minimum interference from government (**laissez-faire**).

Early Federal Government Economic Policies

In the 1790's, there was some government interference. The first Secretary of the Treasury, **Alexander Hamilton**, created regulations to strengthen the U.S. economy. For a long period after that, the Federal Government followed a laissez-faire policy.

Adam Smith had also warned of another danger to a free market economy. He said that unregulated monopolies destroy competition and endanger the freedom of a market economy. Great economic changes swept America in the 19th and 20th Centuries. To help people survive and to preserve fairness, the Federal Government has changed its economic policy.

For example, railroad, banking, and manufacturing monopolies treated farmers roughly in the late 19th Century. Farmers paid high prices for goods, credit, transportation, and supplies. They organized the **Grange Movement** (1867) and the **Populist Party** (1892) to demand help from government. In response, the Federal Government passed the **Interstate Commerce Act** (1887). The act stated "all charges ... shall be fair and reasonable." The act created the **Interstate Commerce Commission** (ICC) that investigated violations of this rule.

Industrial growth changed the country and created a problem for many Americans. They loved economic freedom, but they also knew there was a need for economic stability and fairness.

Exercise 1:

What is the major goal of Federal Government economic policy in a market economy?

[handwritten] ... to encourage free competition

Early 20th Century Policies:
The Progressive Era

Industrialization in the late 19th and early 20th Centuries caused Americans to criticize laissez-faire. They demanded more Federal Government regulation. To battle big business, Americans formed unions, professional organizations, and new political parties. These efforts helped to restore fairness to the market economy.

Political reformers began the **Progressive Movement**. The press helped spread the spirit of progressive reform. **Muckrakers** wrote articles exposing big business' abuse of consumers and workers. Magazines such as *McClure's* featured articles by **Ida Tarbell, Frank Norris, and Lincoln Steffans**. Upton Sinclair's 1906 novel, *The Jungle*, described unsanitary conditions in the Chicago meat packing industry. Muckrakers voiced the public's demand for Federal Government regulation of industry.

On the state level, democratic reforms such as **initiatives, referendums, recalls**, and **secret ballots** gave voters more control over elected officials. States began using their **police powers**. They began to regulate health and safety through factory inspections. They required insurance to cover job accidents. They set rules on minimum employment age, maximum hours for child labor (usually 8-10 hours per day), hours for women, and old age pensions.

On the national level, Progressive reformers such as Robert LaFollette, Theodore Roosevelt, and Woodrow Wilson worked for passage of Federal regulatory laws. Congress passed many laws such as the **Meat Inspection Act**, the **Pure Food and Drug Act**, the **Clayton Anti-Trust Act**, and the **Federal Reserve System**. New amendments were added to the Constitution. The **16th Amendment** created a progressive income tax, and the **17th Amendment** established direct popular election of U.S. Senators.

Exercise 2:

Match the items on the right with groups or government acts on the left.

Set I: Groups

C 1. Farmers

D 2. Monopolists

A 3. Progressives

B 4. Muckrakers

A. restored market fairness
B. exposed industrial problems
C. Grange and Populists
D. eliminated competition

Set II: Regulations

F 5. Federal Interstate Commerce Act

H 6. Federal Clayton Antitrust Act

E 7. Federal Meat Inspection Act

G 8. State maximum hour laws

E. consumer protection
F. control of railroad abuses
G. worker safety
H. control of monopolies

Federal Government Economic Policies
In The Great Depression

It is natural to have recessions and depressions in a market economy. Demand for goods and services, savings, investments, and employment can never be perfectly balanced. A market system allows so much freedom of choice that many factors can cause the economy to change. The terrible collapse of 1929-32 was very different from earlier depressions. It was much worse than ever before, and it touched everyone and everything.

Key Reasons For The Great Crash Of 1929

- Too much wealth was in the hands of only 5-10% of the population.
- American manufacturers were **overproducing** massive amounts of goods.
- **Wages** were not keeping pace with the production and consumer purchasing declined.
- The Harding-Coolidge-Hoover administrations followed **laissez-faire** policies. They refused to "tamper" with income taxes, interest rates, or use economic regulation powers.
- Congress raised **tariffs**. They blocked American markets from other nations. The tariffs were so high it was almost impossible to buy American goods. World trade dried up.

In the Fall of 1929, business declines shook public confidence. Investors panicked, and the unstable economy collapsed. President Hoover's administration continued to follow a laissez-faire policy. The Federal Government did nothing to control big corporations and the rich. By 1932, the gross national product was half what it was in 1929. In those same years, more than five thousand banks closed. Wages, prices, and employment kept dropping.

The collapse bewildered and shocked everyone. At first, most people did not expect the Federal Government to act, but by the election of 1932, people wanted action. The nation turned from Hoover and chose N.Y. Governor **Franklin Delano Roosevelt** in a landslide vote.

FDR and his advisors felt that the Federal Government should **"prime the pump"** (actions to make the consuming public secure and optimistic enough to stimulate spending). Roosevelt and his "New Dealers" focused on three goals: *relief*, *recovery*, and *reform*.

FDR

The New Deal's 3R's

Tactic	Goal	Sample Acts
Relief	• immediate action to stop the economic decline	• Emergency Banking Act, Federal Emergency Relief Act
Recovery	• temporary programs to start economic growth	• Agricultural Adjustment Act, Nat'l Industrial Recovery Act
Reform	• permanent programs to help avoid economic problems	• Federal Deposit Insurance Corp., Social Security Act

The (New Deal) preserved the free enterprise system by remodeling its weakest parts. It also forged a new connection between the individual and the Federal Government. It established the new (Federal Government) role of **stimulator of the economy**.

However, the New Deal ended the policy of laissez-faire. Some economic freedom was lost. There were other negative results, too. Increased Federal spending to finance the New Deal unbalanced the government's budget. **Deficit spending** (heavy borrowing to finance programs) became common. Taxes rose to finance such large government operations. New constitutional questions about stretching of legislative and executive power also arose.

Exercise 3:

Using the clues below, complete the Crossword puzzle on the 3R's.

Across clues
2. FDR's economic policy (2 words)
5. Depression President (initials)
7. "Pump-Priming" goal
8. High _____ helped cause the Depression

Down clues
1. permanent economic change
3. Poor distribution of _____ = cause of Depression
4. immediate aid for severe economic problems
6. programs to move the economy back to normal

Recent Federal Government Economic Policies

Since the Great Depression and World War II, Americans have enjoyed prosperity, but it has not been a smooth ride. There have been economic problems. The role of the U.S. Government in the economy grew tremendously with the Cold War and the growth of population. Lyndon Johnson's Great Society and the Vietnam War created **inflation** (too much Federal Government spending and lagging production causes prices to soar).

By the 1980's, **Ronald Reagan** was trying to reduce the growth of the Federal Government. One Reagan economic policy was the "**New Federalism**." It tried to shift Federal programs in education, health, welfare, and transportation to state and local authorities. The Federal Government eliminated a few programs and reduced others. The states could not finance most of the programs. The Federal Government had to drop the programs or continue spending for them.

Another Reagan economic policy was "**supply side economics**." Reagan hoped a tax cut would free up new investment capital and spur growth to the stagnant economy. He succeeded in getting Congress to pass a 25% reduction in Federal individual and corporate taxes.

The tax cut also reduced government revenue (income). To keep things in balance, severe cuts in Federal Government expenditures were needed. Neither Congress nor the President could agree on enough cuts to keep inflation down. In 1986, Congress passed Reagan's "**tax simplification program**." It simplified payment schedules.

Eventually, supply-side policies did stimulate the economy. At the same time, the Federal Reserve Bank kept inflation under control. However, Reagan's budget cuts hurt millions of poor, handicapped, and homeless people. Critics said that the rich were prospering from the tax cuts at the expense of the lower classes.

A third Reagan economic policy tried to balance the Federal budget. It failed because Reagan tried to restore American military power at the same time. He increased Federal spending and borrowing and drove the Federal deficit to record heights. Currently, the Federal Government spends $100 billion a year just to pay the interest on the $2 trillion national debt.

Responsibility for these deficits must be shared by the President, Congress, and the people. President Bush is working with Congress to reduce the

Ronald Reagan

debt, but they have not been very successful in cutting expenses. Some economists say it can be reduced over time. Others predict it will cause a great economic collapse in the future.

Exercise 4:

Study the cartoon at the right. List three reasons *or* Federal Government actions that make the cartoon's "message" timely and valid. Use the theme "balancing the budget" as your guide.

"Keeping close watch on the Congress."

1. _Failure to balance budget_

2. _Too many tax breaks for wealthy_

3. _Too many poor are starving up to taxes_

Exercise 5:

Use the clues at the bottom of the exercise to fill in the missing words.

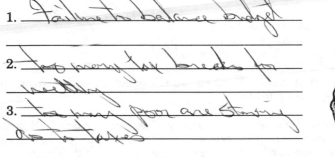

1. _ _ _ _ _ _ _ _ **D**
2. I n v e s t m **E** n t
3.   n e w **F** e d e r a l i s m
4. I n f l a t **I** o n
5.   **C** u t
6.   S **I** d e
7.   **T** a x e s

Clues:
1. a _____ budget avoids deficits and surpluses
2. supply side policy stimulates _____
3. Reagan's program for states to take over Federal programs
4. when too much money chasing too few goods causes prices to rise
5. flaw in Reagan's policy: failure to _____ expenses
6. Policy of lower taxes to stimulate economy is supply _____ policies
7. reduced _____ is the central idea of supply side policies

Additional References On "Economic Policies"

Check your textbook or N&N's *United States History and Government, A Competency Review Text* on:
- The Bank of the United States [pg. 46]
- Tariffs [pgs. 45, 146, 177]
- Federal Government and Labor Unions [pgs. 192, 256]
- Federal Gov't Economic Management of World War I [pgs. 172-173]
- The Great Depression and the New Deal [pgs. 184-197]
- Federal Gov't Economic Management of World War II [pgs. 215, 218]
- The Great Society [pgs. 270-271]
- Reagan's Economic Policies [pgs. 304-306]

Questions

1   Alexander Hamilton's financial plan was one of the first Federal Government's economic policies. Its purpose was to
   1   create a stable economy   3   rebuild the military
   2   balance the budget   4   tax the rich

2   Farmers in the late nineteenth century wanted the Federal Government's economic policies to
   1   get accurate weather reports
   2   control railroads and monopolies
   3   abolish labor unions
   4   pay for modern farm machinery

3   The Progressive Era reformers wanted the Federal Government's economic policies to control
   1   labor unions   3   Muckrakers
   2   monopolies   4   the armed forces

4   Which 1920's situation helped cause the Great Depression?
   1   little Federal economic regulation
   2   low tariffs
   3   unwillingness of people to invest in industry
   4   low industrial production

5   Franklin D. Roosevelt's New Deal policy
   1   strengthened the power of monopolies
   2   promoted laissez faire
   3   broadened the Federal Government's economic role
   4   abolished deficit spending

6   Which idea was behind President Reagan's New Federalism?
   1   Only the Federal Government can provide for citizens' welfare.
   2   Economic problems can be solved by increasing Federal spending.
   3   The Federal Government should return some of its power to states.
   4   The President's military power should be checked by Congress.

7   Which idea is behind the tax reductions of "supply-side economics?"
   1   increase Federal Government spending
   2   decrease industrial production
   3   decrease inflation
   4   increase business investment

8   Opponents of Reagan's economic policies claimed that
      1   the states had too much economic power
      2   the poor and underprivileged were ignored
      3   the President's power grew too fast
      4   military power declined

Essay

Federal Government economic policies have influenced many different groups of people.

Groups

Business
Consumers
Workers
Farmers

Part A

Select *one* group from the list above.

_____

State *one* Federal Government economic policy that influenced this group. [1]

_____

Give *one* way the group was helped or hurt by the policy. [1]

_____

_____

Select *another* group from the list above.

_____

State *one* Federal Government economic policy that influenced this group. [1]

_____

Give *one* way the group was helped or hurt by the policy. [1]

_____

_____

Part B

You should use Part A information in your Part B answer. However, you may include different or additional information in your Part B answer. [6]

Write an essay explaining why Federal Government economic policies have helped or hurt different groups of citizens.

LESSON 7
Major Themes In American Foreign Policy

Since the days of George Washington, the United States has faced problems and conflicts with other nations. Washington warned Americans that their new country was weak. Survival depended on avoiding other nations' problems.

Still, America needed trade. Avoiding Europe's problems was very difficult. Jefferson and Madison became involved in the conflicts of the Napoleonic Period (1800-1815). The United States managed to escape most of Europe's problems in the rest of the 19th Century. Europe was generally peaceful after 1815, and domestic problems were of more concern. Americans focused on slavery, expanding west, and industrializing.

The pattern of non-involvement changed as the 20th Century dawned. Americans fought in two world wars, occupied foreign nations, tried to contain the spread of communism, and became involved in problems in nearly every region of the globe.

Imperialistic Interests: 1890-1914

At the very end of the 19th Century, the United States grew more interested in overseas territory. Industrial nations such as Great Britain, France, Germany, Japan, Belgium, the Netherlands, and Italy were building empires in Africa, the Middle East, Asia, and the Pacific.

There were reasons that industrial nations became **imperialistic** (building vast overseas empires). Commercial and naval ships needed fueling stations. Under-developed lands offered supplies of raw materials needed for industries. They became markets for manufactured goods. There were also missionaries who wished to spread the faith of their homelands to others.

The commercial interests in the United States began reflecting imperialistic desires. Coaling stations were needed in the Pacific. The islands of the Caribbean Sea were of special interest to American sugar companies. They developed plantations on the island of Cuba (a Spanish colony). Spain's harsh rule of the Cuban people led to rebellions. American newspapers covered the Cuban stories. To sell papers, editors stretched the truth. Their sensational style of "creating the news" became known as "**yellow journalism**."

Spain said the conflict was none of our business. Relations between the United States and Spain grew tense. Finally, a mysterious explosion destroyed a U.S. battleship visiting Havana early in 1898. Writers of yellow journalism blamed Spain for the sabotage. They whipped up a public outrage. Groups of Americans demanded war against Spain. Congress yielded to the pressure and declared war.

*In the 1890's,
Uncle Sam "went fishing"
for colonies in the Caribbean.*

President McKinley ordered a blockade and invasion of Cuba. The U.S. Pacific fleet surprised the Spanish in the Philippines. American troops landed in Cuba in the heat of summer. It has been called the worst run American military campaign in history. However, Spain was weak and even less prepared for war than the U.S. Several brilliant naval victories resulted in a quick peace settlement.

As a result of the Spanish American War, the United States took over a small empire of overseas territories. Spain gave up Cuba and Puerto Rico in the Caribbean and the Philippines and Guam in the Pacific. Cuba was directly or indirectly controlled by the U.S. until 1934. The Philippines were given their freedom in 1946. Guam and Puerto Rico remain part of the U.S. today.

As the 20th Century began, the United States had a considerable empire, and interest in foreign trade was growing. President Theodore Roosevelt (1901-1909) extended U.S. overseas influence, especially in Latin America. His blunt use of American power in the Caribbean and Panama became known as the **Big Stick Policy**.

There had always been interest in a canal to connect the Atlantic and Pacific. Roosevelt felt the new island empire had to be connected by a Central American canal. He helped rebels in Panama gain their independence from Colombia in 1903. Panama's new government granted the United States a special zone to build a canal connecting the Atlantic and Pacific Oceans.

The Panama Canal opened in 1914. Having American territory slicing through the middle of Panama has led to problems since that time. In 1977, the U.S. finally agreed to return the Canal Zone to Panama by 1999. However, the U.S. is still deeply involved in Panamanian affairs.

The alleged drug trading and corruption of dictator Manuel Noriega threatened American military bases in the Canal Zone. In December 1989, President Bush sent an invasion force to Panama to protect American interests.

At the turn of the century, McKinley and Roosevelt had to put down fierce rebellions in the Philippines. Intense rivalry also arose over trade in China. American diplomats worked out an "Open Door Policy." Japan and the European powers finally agreed to let the U.S. trade in Chinese ports.

All this imperialist behavior disturbed some Americans. Anti-imperialists pointed to our traditional policy of non-involvement dating back to Washington. Still, the nationalistic feeling in the country outweighed the anti-imperialists. In the long run, U.S. imperialism was basically trade oriented. There was less exploitation of other countries than the British, French, and Germans allowed in Africa and Asia.

Exercise 1:

As the 19th Century closed, the United States took an active interest in overseas territory. List three reasons for this interest.

1. _Trade_
2. _raw materials_
3. _rest areas - stepping points_

Exercise 2:

1. On the map above, circle *three* land areas controlled by the U.S. by the early 20th Century.
2. Which area eventually became a communist country? _Cuba_
3. In which area(s) are the residents U.S. citizens? ~~_____~~ ~~_____~~
   Puerto Rico
4. Which territory is gradually being returned to its people? _____
   Canal Zone

World Wars And Isolation

I WANT YOU
FOR U.S. ARMY
NEAREST RECRUITING STATION

In 1914, Europe plunged into World War I. America avoided European conflicts for nearly a century. The difference in 1914 was that America's position had changed. Americans had considerable trade and investment ties in Europe. President Wilson proclaimed the U.S. neutral, but his actions did not stop interference with our shipping. German submarine attacks increased. Eventually, Congress declared war on the Central Powers in 1917.

America broke the war's stalemate. The military balance tipped in favor of the Allied Powers, and the Central Powers surrendered in late 1918. Wilson tried to guarantee fair treatment for Germany at the **Paris Peace Conference** in 1919. Wilson dreamed of setting up a just peace that would end the use of war in international conflicts.

The final **Treaty of Versailles** largely ignored Wilson's goals. Britain, France, and Italy laid the entire blame for the war on Germany's shoulders. While the treaty's terms were harsh, a few of Wilson's ideas were used. The **League of Nations** came into existence as a world peace organization.

At home, however, isolationism was strong. Wilson's hopes for a lasting peace were blocked by the Senate. It refused to ratify (approve) the Treaty of Versailles. Many Senators felt that belonging to the League of Nations would permanently involve us in Europe's problems. *Did not join L of N*

Isolationism remained strong during the next twenty years. Isolationists wanted the United States to turn its back on European and global affairs. During 1930's, Congress passed a series of **neutrality acts** to keep us out of Europe's rising conflicts.

President Franklin Roosevelt did not believe the United States could hide behind neutrality acts. He said we were too commercially involved with European nations. He wanted to use active diplomacy to settle problems.

Totalitarian nations (Germany, Italy, Japan) began military aggression in the 1930's. Roosevelt wanted to help threatened democracies, but Congress held him back. Congress did not move until Hitler conquered France in 1940. When the Nazis began intense attacks on Britain, Congress passed the **Lend-Lease Act**. The act moved us closer to war. It gave military supplies to Britain and later to the U.S.S.R.

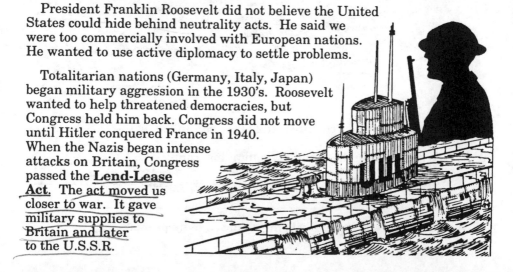

In late 1941, Japan attacked the United States naval base in Hawaii. Congress declared war on the Axis Alliance (Japan, Germany, and Italy). Once again, the U.S. became fully involved in a European war. In the four years that followed, American troops saw action in every part of the globe.

During World War II, President Roosevelt met several times with British Prime Minister Churchill, Soviet Premier Stalin, and other Allied leaders. At these "summit" meetings they worked out the military strategy to defeat the Axis. They decided on post-war national boundaries, new governments, and the fate of colonial empires. They also made plans to create the **United Nations**.

Slowly, the Allies defeated the Axis. Italy fell in 1943. In June of 1944, the Allies launched the largest invasion in history. Thousands of allied troops landed in Normandy. France and Belgium were quickly freed. Germany surrendered in May of 1945. Japan finally surrendered in August 1945 after the U.S. dropped two atomic bombs on its cities.

Exercise 3:

In the 1st half of the 20th Century, U.S. foreign policy actions fit into four categories: **non-involvement**, **international cooperation**, **military action**, and **imperialism**. Write the name of the category into which each event or picture fits.

1. _Military_ — Declaration of War on Germany (1917)

2. _non involvement_ — Congress passes Neutrality Acts (1930's)

3. _military_ — U.S. invades Normandy, France (1944)

4. _imperialism_ — Panama Canal constructed by U.S. (1904-1914)

5. _non involvement_ — Senate refuses membership in the League of Nations

6. _imperialism_ — Big Stick Policy

7. _International cooperation_ — U.S. joins the U.N.

Global Involvement Since 1945

Events at the end of World War II forced the United States to become a world leader. The U.S. did not suffer any direct war damage and its economy was strong. All of the European powers and Japan exhausted their resources in the war. All suffered severe damage. Soviet leader Josef Stalin took advantage of the chaos to spread communism globally.

The United States opposed forcing communism on people against their will. American leaders felt the U.S. was the only nation that could block Stalin. A **Cold War** began between the U.S. and the U.S.S.R. It was a costly conflict, fought through alliances, threats, espionage, foreign aid, and propaganda.

Often, the superpowers gave millions of dollars in aid to strengthen their allies. In 1947, Congress passed the **Marshall Plan**. The Marshall Plan gave money, technicians, and machinery to rebuild the war-damaged economies. In 1949, Congress approved the **NATO Treaty** (North Atlantic Treaty Organization). It became a military shield for Western Europe. It was the first **collective security treaty** (multi-national defense) that the U.S. ever joined. NATO became the key element in the **containment** policy (holding back the aggressive growth of communism). In addition to NATO, the containment policy included:

- **The Truman Doctrine** (1947) - Military aid kept communists from taking Greece and Turkey.

- **The Berlin Airlift** (1948) - The U.S., Britain, and France overcame a Soviet attempt to push them out of Berlin. When the Soviets blockaded land and water access to the city, the Allies supplied Berlin by air for a year.

- **Korean War** (1950-1953) - U.S. led United Nations forces in preventing North Korean communists from taking over South Korea.

- **Vietnam War** (1965-1973) - U.S. attempted to keep North Vietnamese communists from taking over South Vietnam.

 During the Cold War, policy makers believed the U.S. must defeat the **domino theory**. They felt that if we did not help one nation defend against communist aggression, all of the nations of a region would fall.

The major test of the containment policy came in Vietnam. In the 1950's and early 1960's, Presidents Eisenhower and Kennedy sent military advisors to South Vietnam. In 1965, President Johnson sent combat troops. Half a million troops eventually served in Vietnam by the time the war ended under President Nixon.

The length of the war, the loss of lives, and the expense wore down the public's support. The war became increasingly unpopular, and protests mounted. Nixon finally withdrew the last U.S. forces in 1974. Almost all Southeast Asia fell to the communists in the next year.

In the 1970's, Nixon and Secretary of State Kissinger began to change U.S. relations with the communist world. Their policy of **détente** stressed diplomatic negotiations instead of armed confrontations. They reopened diplomatic relations with China and negotiated arms agreements with the Soviets.

In the late 1980's, Soviet leader **Mikhail Gorbachev** began a series of political and economic changes inside the U.S.S.R. He changed foreign policy to reduce Soviet military and political power in Eastern Europe. Poland, Hungary, Czechoslovakia, and Romania ousted communist leaders. East Germans overthrew the communist government, tore down the Berlin Wall, and reunited with West Germany. In the late 1980's and early 1990's, Presidents Reagan and Bush met with Gorbachev. They agreed to cut missiles and troops in Europe. Gorbachev's actions led to the U.S.S.R.'s disintegration in 1991. One of the superpowers self-destructed. The Cold War appeared over.

Exercise 4:

Match the terms in column 2 with the descriptions in column 1.

_G_ 1. an unsuccessful attempt at containment

_F_ 2. a collective security arrangement

_A_ 3. a successful attempt at containment

_C_ 4. effort to rebuild Europe

_E_ 5. blocked communism in Greece and Turkey

_B_ 6. U.S.-Soviet war of words and threats

_H_ 7. belief that if one nation goes communist, its neighbors will fall

_D_ 8. trying to create friendlier relations

A. Korean War
B. Cold War
C. Marshall Plan
D. Détente
E. Truman Doctrine
F. NATO
G. Vietnam War
H. Domino Theory

Exercise 5:

Place the appropriate letter from the time line next to each event.

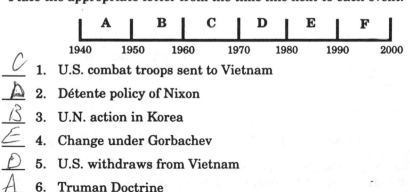

| A | B | C | D | E | F |

1940   1950   1960   1970   1980   1990   2000

_C_ 1. U.S. combat troops sent to Vietnam

_D_ 2. Détente policy of Nixon

_B_ 3. U.N. action in Korea

_E_ 4. Change under Gorbachev

_D_ 5. U.S. withdraws from Vietnam

_A_ 6. Truman Doctrine

_A_ 7. World War II ends

Additional References On "U.S. Foreign Policy"

Check your textbook or N&N's *United States History and Government, A Competency Review Text* on:

- Washington's neutrality [pg. 39]
- The Monroe Doctrine [pg. 41]
- Westward Expansion and Manifest Destiny [pgs. 40-41]
- Annexation of Hawaii [pg. 150]
- Woodrow Wilson: WW I, Neutrality, and Versailles [pgs. 147-150]
- The U.S. and Latin America [pgs. 205, 266-267]
- The Cold War [pgs. 224-226]
- Containment and the Korean War [pgs. 232-233]
- Vietnam War [pgs. 281-285]
- Reagan's policies [pgs. 310-313]

Questions

Base your answer to question 1 on the map below and on your knowledge of social studies.

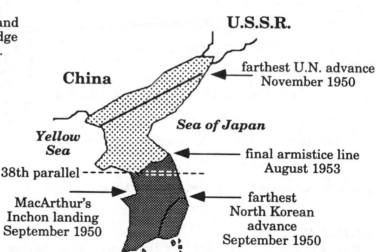

U.S.S.R.

China

farthest U.N. advance
November 1950

Yellow Sea

Sea of Japan

38th parallel

final armistice line
August 1953

MacArthur's
Inchon landing
September 1950

farthest
North Korean
advance
September 1950

1   With which American foreign policy is the map connected?
1   isolationism
2   containment
3   détente
4   imperialism

2   Which was an outward sign of United States imperialism in the early 20th Century?
1   building of the Panama Canal
2   declaring neutrality when World War I broke out
3   rejecting membership in the League of Nations
4   attempting to contain the spread of communism

3   The need for overseas fueling stations for American ships led to which policy?
1   détente
2   containment
3   isolation
4   imperialism

4   Which Senate action was the result of isolationism after World War I?
1   sending combat troops to Vietnam
2   rejecting membership in the League of Nations
3   accepting membership in the United Nations
4   helping to rebuild Western Europe

5   Which goal led to an alliance of the United States and the Soviet Union?
1   containing communism
2   rebuilding Western Europe
3   defeating the Axis Nations
4   building colonial empires

6   Which was the reason President Johnson sent U.S. combat troops into Vietnam in 1965?
1   protection of Middle East oil reserves
2   blocking an invasion by Axis Nations
3   helping the United Nations defend Europe
4   stopping the spread of communism

Essay

In the 20th Century, United States became more involved in global affairs for many reasons.

Reasons

Imperial desires
Aggression of others
Economic interests
Spread of communism
Alliances with others

Part A

Choose *two* reasons from the list above. For *each* reason:
    1)   list *one* specific place where we became involved overseas and
    2)   explain whether involvement in that place helped or hurt the
        United States. [4]

Reasons	Place Involved	How Helped or Hurt?
1. _____	1. _____	1. _____
		_____
		_____
		_____
2. _____	2. _____	2. _____
		_____
		_____
		_____

Part B

You should use Part A information in your Part B answer. However, you may include different or additional information in your Part B answer. [6]

Write an essay explaining global problems and their effect on the United States in the 20th Century.

Issues Facing America In The 1990's

The United States is a great nation because its people constantly struggle to make it a better place to live. This quality attracts immigrants from every part of the globe. America holds the promise of a better life under a democratic system. America chooses leaders democratically, by open and fair elections. Americans work at making their Constitution's promise of basic human rights a reality. The U.S. market economy provides more goods and services than any other nation in the world. Vast opportunities are open to everyone.

Yet, America is not a perfect place. The reality of America has not always lived up to the promise of America. There are still inequalities, poverty, and illiteracy to be overcome, and an environment to be cleaned and preserved. The test of every generation of Americans is always how it preserves what is good about the society while it eliminates what is bad.

Domestic Social Problems

While many Americans have a high standard of living, some still suffer in poverty. Since the days of the Great Depression, American government has tried to help the underprivileged.

The Homeless

During the 1970's and 1980's, the cost of housing rose sharply. Not everyone could afford high rents and mortgages. The number of homeless people increases daily. This is especially true in urban areas. State and local governments are unable or unwilling to help the homeless find permanent housing. Many homeless people live in temporary shelters in the streets and parks.

Cost of housing is one reason for the increase in homeless Americans.

Special Interests
Lobby For
No More Cuts

The Poor

Homelessness is only one sign of poverty. Most of the nation's poor have housing, but it is substandard. The poor also suffer from inadequate education that limits their job opportunities. They have little or no medical care. Crime and drugs infest poor neighborhoods.

Federal, state, and local governments spend billions of dollars to help the poor. There are many examples of government programs. **Headstart** helps poor children prepare for school. **Medicaid** helps pay medical bills. Low income housing projects have been built.

Retraining programs teach new job skills to the unemployed. There are hundreds of programs, but there is never enough money to help everyone. These programs help the poor to survive, but they do not allow families to break out of their poverty. As children are born into poor families, increased expenses make it more difficult to survive. For some families, the cycle of poverty continues from generation to generation.

The Children

There is also a growing problem over child care. The number of working parents, especially single parents, is rising. They are finding it hard to find safe, affordable care for their young children. Poor families suffer most from this problem. Some of the larger private companies are providing work site day care centers for their employees' children. Increasing numbers of people are looking for low cost government sponsored day care facilities.

Opponents fear the cost is too great for the already burdened taxpayer. Yet, if parents cannot work, the standard of living will decline. If this happens, poverty increases, and taxpayers will have to bear the burden of increased welfare costs. As with other social problems, there are no easy, low cost answers.

The Elderly

Poverty threatens the middle class too. As people grow older and retire, they find their savings, pensions, and Social Security allowances cannot cover their costs of living. High medical costs and nursing home fees quickly wipe out savings. The Federal Government provides Medicare assistance, but costs are rising so fast that there is doubt whether it can continue. The problems will grow worse as the number of elderly doubles in the 21st Century.

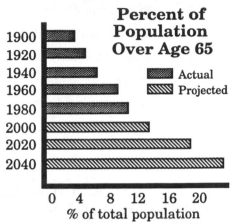

Percent of Population Over Age 65

% of total population

The AIDS Epidemic

An even more pressing social problem is the AIDS epidemic. AIDS results from a viral infection which breaks down the human immune system. The infection is usually fatal. Scientists have not yet been able to find a cure or a vaccine to prevent the disease. The virus spreads through the transfer of body fluids in unprotected sexual activity and through the use of contaminated needles shared by both recreational and "hard-core" drug users. Getting AIDS through a blood transfusion is extremely rare.

While it is almost impossible to contract AIDS except as noted above, many Americans fear people with the disease. They refuse to go to school or work with those who test positive for HIV (the virus that causes AIDS). AIDS patients are subject to considerable discrimination. There are laws intended to prevent this inequality. Although the Federal Government is educating the public about the disease, the problems continue as the disease spreads.

Exercise 1:

On the line to the left of each statement, write whether it is a "fact" or an "opinion."

_____ 1. Medicaid programs help the poor with medical expenses.

_____ 2. The Federal Government is not doing enough for the poor.

_____ 3. Housing costs rose sharply in most places in the U.S. in the 1980's.

_____ 4. The percentage of elderly as a portion of the population more than doubled since 1900.

_____ 5. Currently, there is no vaccine for the virus that causes AIDS.

_____ 6. Free health care provided by the Federal Government would
           result in longer life for humans.

_____ 7. Currently, AIDS is considered a fatal disease.

_____ 8. Working mothers would get higher paying jobs if the Federal
           Government provided day care for their children.

_____ 9. The need for day care centers increased in recent years as more
           mothers have entered the workforce.

_____ 10. Headstart is a Federal program that helps poor children
           prepare for school.

America And Global Issues

Events in other parts of the world strongly influence the United States. The actions of people and governments in Latin America, Europe, Africa, Asia, and the Middle East influence Americans daily.

The Trade Imbalance

The global economy changed greatly in the last half century. After World War II, the United States became the number one provider of high quality goods and services in the world. Western Europe and Japan rebuilt their economies using new technology and research. Combined with lower labor costs and government protection, these nations once again became competitive with the United States.

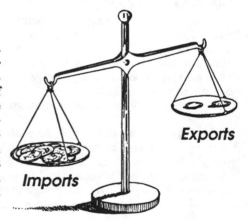

Exports

Imports

Being on top for so many years without serious competition, American industries were slow to invest in new production methods. They did not spend as much as they should have on product research and improvement. In the 1970's, the U.S. began to feel serious foreign competition in electronics and automobiles.

In the 1980's, foreign competition challenged America's position as the world's primary economic power. American firms lost a hefty share of the global markets they had once dominated. U.S. companies still export large quantities of food, chemicals, and high tech equipment, but their share of world markets is shrinking. In 1965, the United States provided 15% of the world's goods. Twenty years later, it was providing less than 10%. Japan now exports a higher percentage of its goods than the United States.

At the same time, world population grew and so did global demand for goods and services. The need for raw materials made American industries increasingly dependent on other nations. Foreign manufacturers also competed for scarce raw materials, driving prices and production costs up.

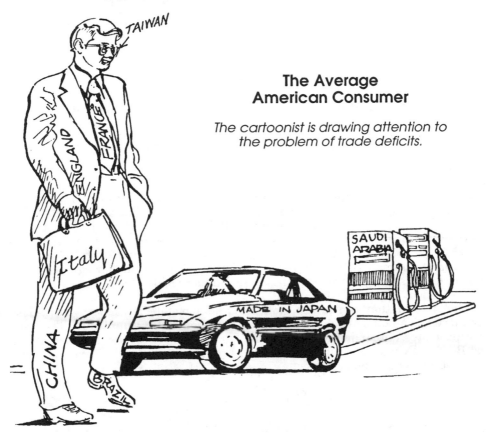

The Average
American Consumer

The cartoonist is drawing attention to the problem of trade deficits.

America now depends on Venezuela, Nigeria, Mexico, and the Middle East for half its petroleum. Foreign countries make almost half of the automobile parts used in the United States. We import more than one-fourth of the electronic equipment we use. One-fifth of our food comes from other countries.

All this change worries economists. Every year for the past decade, the United States has shown a **trade deficit**. This means it imports (buys) more from foreign countries than it exports (sells) to them. Money spent for foreign goods is money draining out of the U.S. When this happens, business declines here and unemployment rises.

Solutions are not easy. Trade restriction laws, such as **quotas** and high **tariffs** designed to protect U.S. industry, often backfire when other countries **reciprocate** (retaliate) by restricting U.S. imports. The hard fact is that U.S. firms have to spend more of their income on new equipment, product research, and worker training to restore the competitive edge.

Exercise 2:

Use the clues below
to find missing words.

1. _T_ _E_ _N_
2. _r e c i p_ _R_ _i c a t e_
3. _M_ _A_ _r k e t_
4. _____ _D_ _____
5. _R e s_ _E_ _a r c h_

Clues:

1. In the last 20 years, America's share of the world's business dropped from 15% to ____ %.
2. If we raise tariffs to protect our home industries, other nations ____.
3. America no longer has the same share of the world's ____.
4. When a country's imports exceed its exports, it has a trade ____.
5. To be competitive, American companies have to invest more in ____.

Human Rights

In many parts of the world, tyranny destroys basic freedoms. As the world's leading democratic nation, the United States wishes to see freedom enjoyed by all people. It strongly supports the ideals written in the **United Nations Charter**, and the U.N.'s *Universal Declaration of Human Rights*. In 1975, the U.S. joined 35 nations in signing the **Helsinki Accord** to promote human rights. It is a fundamental part of our foreign policy to speak out against governments that deny human rights.

One nation that constantly violates human rights is South Africa. The country has an official policy of racial segregation called **apartheid**. This policy promotes discrimination, inequality, and injustice. Under the leadership of Bishop Desmond Tutu and Nelson Mandela, black South Africans have worked to change the system.

The United States condemns apartheid, but South Africa is an important trading partner, and this has softened official government criticisms of the racial policy. Various groups in the U.S. have put tremendous pressure on the U.S. government to take a stronger stand against apartheid. Some Americans want to break relations with South Africa. Others want U.S. corporations to **divest** (give up) their business interests in South Africa. Divesting puts severe economic pressure on South Africa but has also led to a loss of jobs for blacks.

During the Cold War struggle, the U.S. frequently criticized China, Cuba, Cambodia, and "Iron Curtain" countries for violating human rights. Communist powers and dictatorships still ignore human rights treaties such as the **Helsinki Accords** (1975).

Exercise 3:
Fill in the blanks.

1. Defending __human__ __rights__ is a basic part of U.S. foreign policy.

2. Promotion of human rights is also a basic idea of the __Helsinki__

   Accord and the Charter of the _____ _____ .

3. The policy of __apartheid__ in South Africa denies equality to blacks.

4. The U.S. Government has not been as forceful as it could be in opposing apartheid because of strong __economic__ ties to South Africa.

5. Some groups are trying to get U.S. companies to __divest__ business interests in South Africa.

The Environment
America uses enormous amounts of energy. Alternatives have been sought for the traditional fuels of oil and coal. Nuclear power has been one such option. Close to 100 nuclear power plants operate in the United States, producing relatively clean and efficient energy. However, few new reactors have been built in recent years because nuclear power has become controversial. Public fears about accidents releasing radiation, tremendous costs (over four billion dollars) of building new reactors, and the problem of the disposal of radioactive waste have created negative feelings.

American society is constantly changing through technological innovations. Unfortunately, much of this technological advancement has come at a high cost to the environment. Factory and automobile emissions have caused the problem of **acid rain** (contaminated rainwater falls hundreds of miles from the source).

Many of the waterways throughout America have been filled with harmful chemicals. Other chemicals are contributing to the deterioration of the protective ozone layer surrounding the earth. Landfills are overflowing, and communities are running out of room as the amount of trash generated by Americans grows daily.

Environmentalists also express concern over the misuse of natural resources and destruction of land. Roads, shopping centers, and housing are built over former farms and forests. Strip mining tears up large chunks of earth in attempts to find minerals. Solutions are not easily found. Those who want to protect the environment must compete with the demands of the American consumer.

The Federal Government established the **Environmental Protection Agency** (EPA) and a "super fund" to clean up old waste sites, but the ultimate answers may cause radical alterations to the nation's lifestyle in the decades to come.

Exercise 4:

Using two or three sentences, discuss the theme of the cartoon.

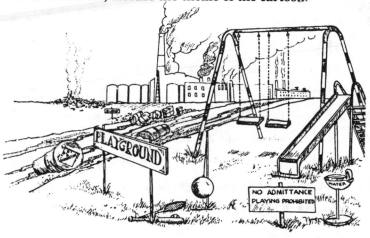

_____

_____

_____

_____

Additional References On
"Issues Facing America In The 1990's"

Check your textbook or N&N's *United States History and Government, A Competency Review Text* on:

- Abortion [pg. 306]
- Farmers [pg. 306]
- The handicapped [pg. 300]
- Immigration [pg. 307]
- Nuclear power [pgs. 242-243]
- Technology [pg. 243]
- Terrorism [pg. 311]
- Ecological concerns [pgs. 272, 280, 282, 289]

Questions

1 Which explains why the U.S. currently has a foreign trade deficit?
   1   State governments spend too much money.
   2   Few countries sell their goods in the United States.
   3   American goods are not available for export.
   4   America is importing more than it is exporting.

2 The United States Government is against the apartheid policy of South Africa's government because it
   1   has resulted in religious wars
   2   violates basic human rights
   3   creates a major trade deficit
   4   fails to contain communism

Base your answer to questions 3 and 4 on the graph below and on your knowledge of social studies.

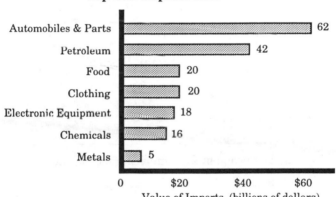

Top U.S. Imports 1988

3 Which statement can be proven from the information given in the graph?
   1   The total value of our exports exceeds that of our imports.
   2   Multinational firms are becoming less powerful.
   3   The value of petroleum imports is more than twice that of food.
   4   Trade restrictions severely limit clothing imports.

4 For which products is America most dependent on the foreign countries?
   1   electronics and chemicals
   2   food and clothing
   3   chemicals and metals
   4   petroleum and automotive products

5 In the future, the growing numbers of elderly people will
   1   greatly strain the Social Security system
   2   make the Federal Government take over public schools
   3   demand day care facilities for children
   4   raise the trade deficit

6   The problem of growing numbers of homeless Americans is partly due
      to
      1   rapidly rising housing costs
      2   the collapse of the Medicare system
      3   poor architectural designs in public housing
      4   lack of qualified construction workers

7   Since there is no known cure for AIDS, the major approach of the
      Federal Government has been to
      1   educate the public about how it is spread
      2   segregate people with AIDS
      3   deny AIDS patients equal rights
      4   vaccinate children

Essay

American society faces a number of serious issues in the 1990's.

Issues

Poverty	AIDS
Child Care	Balance of Trade
Elderly	Human Rights

Part A

Select *one* issue from the list above.

_____

Explain why this issue is a problem for American society. [2]

_____

_____

Select *another* issue from the list above.

_____

Explain why this issue is a problem for American society. [2]

_____

_____

Part B

You should use Part A information in your Part B answer. However, you
may include different or additional information in your Part B answer. [6]

**Write an essay explaining two serious problems American society
must solve in the 1990's.**

Practice Competency Test

Your success on the Competency Test depends very much on <u>how</u> you take the test. Here are some suggestions for taking this practice Competency Test and the Competency Test itself:

1. Give Yourself Some Time to Warm Up.
Skim over the whole test. Put your Part 1 answers on scrap paper. When you get to Part 2, read the questions and jot down on scrap paper any facts you think you might use. Do this for *each* question on Part 2. It will help you to decide which *two* questions to choose.

2. Read Part 1 Again, But More Slowly This Time.
Look for ideas you might use on Part 2 essays. Jot them down on your scrap paper.

3. Write a Part 2 Essay.
Choose the one you feel most confident about and write the Part B answer on your scrap paper. Remember:

- use facts and ideas listed in Part A, but add more information
- if a topic sentence is given, use it as your beginning
- explain the ideas fully and clearly

4. Go Back to Part 1.
Work on the questions that you left blank.

5. Write the Other Part 2 Essay.
Do it on your scrap paper. Use the same care you did when you wrote the first essay.

6. Wait While the Proctor Checks Your Paper.
Sometimes they notice blanks or parts you left out.

Practice U.S. History Competency Test
Part 1
Answer All 50 Questions

1   A government system which divides power between states and the national government is
1   precedent   3   federalism
2   totalitarian   4   capitalist

2   Which is a basic principle of the *Declaration of Independence*?
1   Rulers receive their power directly from God.
2   People cannot be trusted to govern themselves.
3   People do not have the right to rebel against a government.
4   Government receives its power from the consent of the governed.

3   The first use of the amendment process in the United States Constitution resulted in the
1   Supreme Court using judicial review
2   adoption of the Bill of Rights
3   Federal Government establishing political parties
4   President vetoing an act of Congress

4   The process of amending the Constitution allows the Federal Government to
1   correct the mistakes of state governors
2   add to the power of local government
3   meet changing situations
4   create an Unwritten Constitution

5   The Presidential Cabinet, political parties, and judicial review developed through
1   Constitutional amendments
2   political traditions
3   Congressional laws
4   Supreme Court order

Base your answer to question 6 on the headlines below and on your knowledge of social studies.

HOUSE OF REPRESENTATIVES MOVES TO IMPEACH PRESIDENT
SENATE APPROVES APPOINTMENT OF NEW CHIEF JUSTICE
SUPREME COURT UPHOLDS CONGRESSIONAL LAW

6   Which basic idea of the United States Government is best illustrated by the headlines?
1   federalism
2   electoral college system
3   system of checks and balances
4   process of amending the Constitution

7 In a republic, the people
1 make all decisions directly
2 elect officials to make decisions
3 follow the leadership of a hereditary monarch
4 follow the leadership of a single party

8 Which statement reflects the idea of "due process?"
1 The electoral college chooses the President.
2 Bills must go through both houses of Congress to become laws.
3 The Supreme Court can declare laws unconstitutional.
4 Citizens accused of crimes are assured proper and equal legal procedures.

9 Which best explains why there are political parties in the U.S.?
1 The United States Constitution established political parties.
2 Political parties formed to reflect people's different points of view and interests.
3 The Supreme Court, using judicial review, established political parties.
4 Congress passed a law providing for the formation of political parties.

10 The system of racial segregation in the South after the Civil War was similar to
1 apartheid in South Africa   3 antitrust legislation
2 communism in China   4 integration

11 Which condition was common during the Age of Industrialization in the United States?
1 Most workers belonged to labor unions.
2 Women were not allowed to work in any factories.
3 Workers received low wages and worked long hours.
4 Government policies protected the rights of workers.

12 Labor unions were formed mainly to
1 secure better working conditions and wages for workers
2 select political candidates to run for office
3 allow workers to buy the factories from the owners
4 serve as social clubs for the workers

13 Which situation in the United States is most likely to lead to a nativist reaction against immigrants?
1 an increase in the standard of living
2 a decrease in unemployment figures
3 depressed economic conditions
4 an increase in government social welfare policies

14 A major difference between the immigrants to the United States at the beginning of the 20th century and immigrants of today is
1 the earlier immigrants settled in more rural areas
2 most of today's immigrants do not come from Europe
3 the later immigrants did not meet with prejudice
4 the earlier immigrants could not find unskilled jobs

Base your answers to questions 15 through 17 on the map below and on your knowledge of social studies.

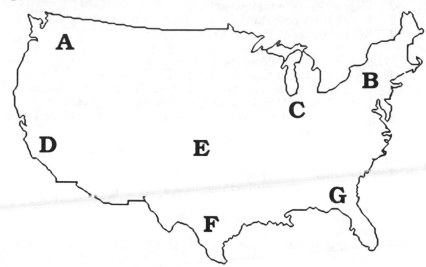

15   Which letter indicates a region that had the major ports of entry for European immigrants during the early 20th century?
1   A   3   C
2   B   4   D

16   Which two letters represent the areas where the greatest industrialization occurred during the late 19th and early 20th centuries?
1   A and D   3   B and C
2   D and E   4   F and G

17   Which letter represents the last settled area in the lower United States?
1   A   3   E
2   D   4   F

_____

18   United States' control over Cuba, Puerto Rico, Guam, and the Philippines at the end of the 19th Century was seen by some as
1   neutrality   3   socialism
2   détente   4   imperialism

19   The Populist Party campaigned to have government control railroads and monopolies in the late 19th century. It was led by
1   farmers   3   city political bosses
2   big business   4   immigrants

20   Progressive Era reformers were aided by Muckrakers who used the power of
1   labor unions   3   mass media
2   monopolies   4   third parties

Base your answers to questions 21 and 22 on the cartoon below and on your knowledge of social studies

21   Which group would strongly disagree with the cartoonist's viewpoint?
1   industrialists
2   farmers
3   factory workers
4   urban dwellers

22   The cartoonist believes that during the Age of Industrialization the U.S. Senate was
1   less effective in dealing with big business than the House of Representatives
2   passing strong legislation to control big business
3   more powerful than the Presidency
4   being run and taken advantage of by big business

23   The main goal of the Progressive Movement of the early 20th Century was to
1   improve the economic condition of the farmers in the United States
2   reform government and control the abuses of big business
3   encourage the abusive tactics of big business
4   protect the United States from the communist threat

24   In the United States, income taxes are used
1   only by the Federal Government
2   only by state governments
3   by local, state, and Federal Governments
4   only to support education

Base your answers to questions 25 and 26 on chart below and on your knowledge of social studies.

Ten Largest Cities in the United States	
1860	**1900**
1. New York (814,669) 2. Philadelphia (565,529) 3. Baltimore (212,418) 4. Boston (177,840) 5. New Orleans (168,675) 6. Cincinnati (161,044) 7. St. Louis (160,773) 8. Chicago (109,260) 9. Buffalo (81,129) 10. Newark (71,941)	1. New York (3,437,202) 2. Chicago (1,698,575) 3. Philadelphia (1,293,697) 4. St. Louis (575,238) 5. Boston (560,892) 6. Baltimore (508,957) 7. Cleveland (381,768) 8. Buffalo (352,387) 9. San Francisco (342,782) 10. Cincinnati (325,902)

25   Based on the chart, which statement is accurate? Between 1860 and 1900,
1   most Americans left the cities
2   industrialization forced many people to leave the cities to find work
3   the population of west coast cities was greater than east coast cities
4   newer inland cities grew faster than older eastern coastal cities

26   Based on the chart, which conclusion is true?
1   By 1900 the United States was becoming increasingly urbanized.
2   By 1900 west coast port cities were becoming more important than east coast trading ports.
3   New York City served only as a stopover point for most of the immigrants coming into the United States.
4   Railroad development had little impact upon the development of cities.

---

27   At the end of World War I, the United States Senate refused membership in the League of Nations because
1   there was a desire among Senators for isolationism
2   the United States was already in the United Nations
3   the League was dominated by communist countries
4   the Supreme Court declared the League unconstitutional

28   One cause of the Great Depression was that government followed too closely the economic policy of
1   tight regulation of business
2   cutting taxes
3   deficit spending
4   laissez-faire

29 Franklin D. Roosevelt's New Deal established the economic policy that government should act as a

1 protector of monopolies   3 stimulator in a sluggish economy
2 promoter of laissez - faire   4 balancer of the budget

30 The United States entered World War II because of
1 an explosion of a U.S. battleship in Havana
2 an air attack on a Pacific naval base
3 an invasion of the Panama Canal
4 North Korea's invasion of South Korea

Base your answer to question 31 on the headlines below and on your knowledge of social studies.

ROOSEVELT SEIZES MONTGOMERY WARD COMPANY: ORDERS WAR LABOR BOARD TO RUN COMPANY

OFFICE OF PRICE ADMINISTRATION SETS LIMIT ON RENTS

GOVERNMENT ORDERS EMPLOYERS TO WITHHOLD TAXES FROM WORKERS WAGES

31 The headlines indicate that during World War II, the government economic policy shifted toward
1 a market system   3 laissez-faire
2 neutrality   4 a command system

32 One sign of a change in traditional United States foreign policy after World War II was
1 involvement in permanent military alliances
2 refusal to join the United Nations
3 trade with Europe was begun
4 large scale relief aid was sent to communist countries

Base your answers to questions 33 and 34 on the speakers' statements below and on your knowledge of social studies

Speaker A: Communism is a great threat to American society. It must be stopped at all costs!

Speaker B: It is not in the best interests of the United States to continue fighting in Vietnam. Will it really matter if these poor people adopt a Marxist government?

Speaker C: While we do not always agree with the way communist nations treat their people, world peace is better served if we try to get along with them.

33 Which speaker(s) would be the strongest supporter of the containment policy?
1 A   3 B and C
2 B   4 all of them

34 Which speakers would be the strongest supporter of the détente policy?
1 A and B   3 A and C
2 B and C   4 all of them

35   Which policy marked a change in U.S. relations with the Soviet Union?
1   Theodore Roosevelt's Big Stick Policy
2   William McKinley's Open Door Policy
3   Woodrow Wilson's Fourteen Points
4   Richard Nixon's Détente Policy

36   A result of the Vietnam War was that the United States Government
1   ended foreign aid to all nations
2   cut off trade with all Asian nations
3   became cautious about using military forces
4   placed strict limits on foreign immigration

Base your answers to questions 37 and 38 on the graph at the right and on your knowledge of social studies

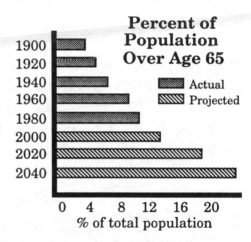

Percent of Population Over Age 65

37   In the period between 1980-2040, the percent of the population over 65 will
1   be cut in half   3   triple
2   double   4   remain stable

38   Which of the following causes the trend indicated on the graph?
1   Most of the new immigrants are older people.
2   The population is shifting from north to south.
3   U.S. infant mortality is higher than that of most nations.
4   Major advances have been made in medicine and health care.

39   Executive - Legislative relations during the Watergate Scandal reflect
1   checks and balances   3   laissez-faire
2   cooperation   4   abuse of judicial review

40   American military action in Korea in the 1950's and in Vietnam in the 1960's were attempts to
1   increase United States trade in Asia
2   free American hostages
3   abolish European imperialism
4   stop the spread of communism

Base your answer to question 41 on the list of Supreme Court Cases below and on your knowledge of social studies.

Dred Scott v. Sandford (1857)
Plessy v. Ferguson (1896)
Brown v. Board of Education (1954)
Bakke v. California (1978)

41   All of these cases involved the issue of
1   racial discrimination
2   the limits of Presidential power
3   judicial review of Congressional laws
4   abortion rights

42   In the past 15 years, massive government borrowing has led to the problem of
1   budget surpluses   3   budget deficits
2   reduced tax revenues   4   reduced services

43   As a result of the Progressive Movement, the New Deal, and the Great Society, the United States Government
1   adopted a laissez-faire economic policy
2   added more economic regulations
3   rejected all forms of socialism
4   reduced taxes

44   Primary elections and conventions are ways United States political parties
1   choose candidates   3   pay taxes
2   make laws   4   raise money

45   To stimulate investment and growth in the economy, those who believe in "supply-side" economics policies want to
1   raise government spending
2   decrease industrial production
3   promote inflation
4   cut taxes

46   Which is an example of interdependence among nations?
1   Chinese troops are ordered to crush a student rights demonstration
2   U.S. Department of Agriculture urges farmers to reduce production
3   U.S. oil imports have risen in the last 10 years
4   Federal officials decide to reduce the number of immigrants admitted

47   Which current economic problem did the the United States Government also face in the Great Depression?
1   the collapse of numerous banks
2   declining union membership
3   reducing the Federal Government's budget surplus
4   high inflation

Base your answers to questions 48 and 49 on the map below and on your knowledge of social studies.

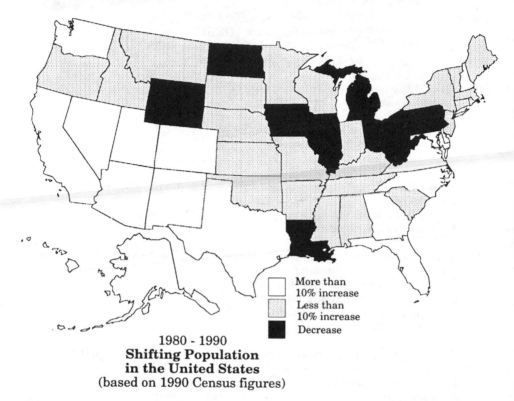

1980 - 1990
**Shifting Population
in the United States**
(based on 1990 Census figures)

Legend:
More than 10% increase
Less than 10% increase
Decrease

48   In which region did the states have the largest population gain?
  1   North East   3   Central Plains
  2   South and Southwest   4   Midwest

49   The most immediate result of the population shifts of the last ten years shown on the map will be a change in the number of
  1   Supreme Court judges appointed
  2   seats in the U.S. Senate of some states
  3   military bases in some states
  4   seats in the House of Representatives assigned some states

_____

50   In the last 30 years, job discrimination against women and minorities has been lessened by
  1   Congressional legislation
  2   Constitutional amendments
  3   sexual harassment
  4   minimum wage laws

Part 2
Answer TWO Questions From This Part

DIRECTIONS: Write your answer to Part A on this page. Write your answer to Part B on the back of this page.

Essay Question 1
All citizens of the United States have a right to equal treatment under the law.

Groups

Women
African Americans
Hispanics
Native Americans

Part A
Select *one* group from the list above. _____

State *one* example of that group experiencing discrimination. [1]

_____

Give *one* way this group achieved greater equality. [1]

_____

_____

Select *another* group from the list above. _____

State *one* example of that group experiencing discrimination. [1]

_____

Give *one* way this group achieved greater equality. [1]

_____

_____

Part B
You should use Part A information in your Part B answer. However, you may include different or additional information in your Part B answer. [6]

Write an essay explaining how different groups have achieved greater equality in the United States.

Essay:

_____

_____

_____

_____

_____

_____

_____

_____

_____

_____

_____

_____

_____

_____

_____

_____

_____

_____

_____

_____

_____

_____

_____

_____

_____

_____

Essay Question 2

Americans desire economic freedom but also want the government to promote economic stability, growth, and fairness.

Government Economic Policies

Regulation of Railroads in the late 19th Century
Antitrust laws in the Progressive Era
Stimulating the economy in the New Deal
Tax Reduction in the 1980's

Part A
Choose *two* policies from the list above. For *each*, state *one* group that has been affected by this policy and give *one* way the group was helped or hurt by the policy. [4]

Policy	Group	How Helped or Hurt
1_____	1_____	1 _____
		_____
		_____
2_____	2_____	2 _____
		_____
		_____

Part B
You should use Part A information in your Part B answer. However, you may include different or additional information in your Part B answer. [6]

Write an essay explaining why different government economic policies have helped or hurt the people.

Essay:

Essay Question 3

The population of many of the United States cities, especially those on the east coast, increased tremendously during the Age of Industrialization, from 1865-1920.

Part A

State *two* reasons why this population growth occurred at this time. [2]

1 _____

_____

2 _____

_____

State *two* effects this population growth had on the cities. [2]

1 _____

_____

2 _____

_____

Part B

You should use Part A information in your Part B answer. However, you may include different or additional information in your Part B answer. [6]

Write an essay discussing why the cities of the United States grew during the second half of the 19th Century through the 1920's and what effects that growth had on these cities.

Essay:

_____
_____
_____
_____
_____
_____
_____
_____
_____
_____
_____
_____
_____
_____
_____
_____
_____
_____
_____
_____
_____
_____
_____
_____
_____
_____
_____
_____
_____
_____

Essay Question 4
Since the end of world War II, the United States society has experienced a variety of significant trends

Trends
Higher urban crime rates
Longer life expectancy
Increased college enrollment of minority students
Increased productivity of farmers

Part A
Choose *two* trends from the list above. For *each*, state *one* cause of the trend, and *one* result of the trend. [4]

Trend	Cause of the Trend	Result of the Trend
1_____	1_____	1_____
_____	_____	_____
		_____
2_____	2_____	2_____
_____	_____	_____
		_____

Part B
You should use Part A information in your Part B answer. However, you may include different or additional information in your Part B answer. [6]

Write an essay explaining why certain trends in modern U.S. society have occurred and what has been the result of the trend.

Essay:

_____

_____

_____

_____

_____

_____

_____

_____

_____

_____

_____

_____

_____

_____

_____

_____

_____

_____

_____

_____

_____

_____

_____

_____

_____

_____

_____

LESSON 10

Last Minute Review Exercises

The Last Minute Review is a set of worksheets based on Lesson 1 through Lesson 8. Completing the worksheets should help you remember the main ideas that have been presented.

The charts are designed so that you can use them yourself, with a study partner, or in a group. (Schools sometimes sponsor special review classes the day before or the morning of the test.) It is suggested that you work with others, because hearing yourself or others talk about the material will build your confidence just before the Competency Test.

If you work alone, it is suggested that you not try to do all of the exercises at one time. Do one at a time and take a break after each. Let the ideas "sink-in."

Answers are included for each worksheet. Looking for the answers as you complete each exercise will help you make important connections. If an idea is not clear, look back at the material in that lesson.

Another technique is to cover the answers and try to fill in the blanks with your own responses. After completing the exercise, compare your responses with the answers given. When you are studying with others, discuss which of your answers is correct and why.

Most students are nervous just before any important test. Trying to "cram" and memorize lists of data and vocabulary is unproductive at this point. To relieve the "last minute jitters," it is better to think and talk about natural connections among major ideas. These exercises are designed to help you see "the big picture" and avoid frustration.

1. The Constitution Framework Of American Government

Part A. Complete the following chart by choosing the appropriate term from the list of answers below.

Terms	Definition
_____	• division of power between the national and the state governments
_____	• governmental powers are split so that no one official, branch, or level becomes too powerful
_____	• government officials are chosen directly and indirectly by citizens' votes
_____	• Federal courts can review the constitutionality of governmental laws and actions
_____	• political traditions and judicial decisions not officially recognized in the Constitution
_____	• ability of each branch of government to monitor the power of the others

Answers

Checks and balances	Judicial review
Federalism	Precedents
Limited government	Representative government

Part B. Time Line — Label the boxes on the time line with the terms below.

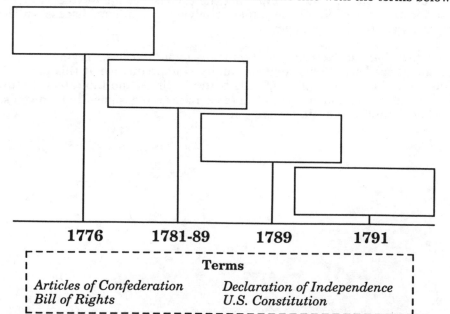

1776   1781-89   1789   1791

Terms

Articles of Confederation	Declaration of Independence
Bill of Rights	U.S. Constitution

2. Separation Of Powers

Part A. Background

Many ideas for our Constitution came in part from the European _____.

English thinkers such as _____ had powerful influence on the members

of the Constitutional Convention. Baron de _____ ideas on _____

of power led the authors of the Constitution to construct a government with

three branches. These include the lawmaking branch or _____,

the enforcement branch headed by the _____, and the interpretive

branch or _____. These three branches may limit the power of each

other in a process known as _____ and _____.

```
┌─────────────────────────────────────────────────────────┐
│                         Answers                           │
│  balances         Enlightenment         Montesquieu's     │
│  checks           judiciary             President         │
│  Congress         Locke                 separation        │
└─────────────────────────────────────────────────────────┘
```

Part B. One Branch as Most Powerful

At various times in the history of the United States, one branch has wielded
more power than other. Often this depends upon the personalities in those
offices and the events they face. Complete the boxes below. *(answers are
found on page 106.)*

Time Period	Strong Branch	Major Events	Proof of Power
1800-1830	Judicial	Testing of Federal v. State Power	
1861-1865	Executive		Abraham Lincoln engaged in controversial actions (e.g.: suspending habeas corpus)
1865-1877	Legislative		Andrew Johnson's problems with the Radical Congress led to impeachment
1933-1945	Executive		
1963-1969	Executive		

Part B Answers

Civil War

FDR got his New Deal programs easily through Congress (in the beginning): commander-in-chief during WW II

Great Depression / World War II

Great Society / Vietnam Conflict

Lyndon Johnson expanded military powers of the President with the Gulf of Tonkin Resolution and Civil Rights legislation

Marshall Court's decisions strengthened national government

Reconstruction

Part C. Limits at Work

The process of checks and balances does not allow one branch to become supreme. Although one branch may exert more authority than the others for a period of time, there is usually action taken to limit that authority. To illustrate this point complete the matching exercise below.

Events	Checks and Balances at Work
first New Deal laws are passed quickly by Congress	
FDR sought to challenge the membership of the Supreme Court	
Woodrow Wilson negotiates the Treaty of Versailles	
Andrew Johnson differs with Congress on how to bring the Confederate states back into the Union during Reconstruction	
Congress passes the War Powers Resolution	

Part C Answers

Congress refuses to change number of Court justices

President is impeached

President Nixon vetoes

Senate refuses to ratify

Supreme Court declares a number of New Deal laws to be unconstitutional

3. Protection Of Constitutional Rights And Liberties

Study the following outline. Choose the correct item from the list of terms below to fill in the blanks.

I. Basic belief: Government serves the people.

A. Source: Jefferson's _____ .

B. _____: Written guarantee against _____ .

C. _____ making citizens aware of precious rights.

```
┌────────────────────────────────────────────────┐
│                   Answers                        │
│  Bill of Rights                 public education │
│  Declaration of Independence    tyranny          │
└────────────────────────────────────────────────┘
```

II. Three methods of expanding rights in America.

A. _____ clarify questions about our rights.

1. In *Miranda v. Arizona* police must read accused persons their rights to ensure _____ of law under the 5th Amendment.

2. _____ said racial segregation in public education violates the 14th Amendment.

3. *Engle v. Vitale:* A state cannot dictate _____ because it violates the 1st Amendment.

```
┌────────────────────────────────────────────────┐
│                   Answers                        │
│  Brown v. Board of Ed.     religious exercises   │
│  due process               Supreme Court decisions│
└────────────────────────────────────────────────┘
```

B. _____ specify procedures and penalties to administer rights fairly.

1. Civil Rights Acts of 1957, 1960, 1964, and 1968 enforced the ideal of equality for _____ .

2. _____ set penalties against violations of the 15th Amendment.

```
┌────────────────────────────────────────────────┐
│                   Answers                        │
│  Congressional laws    Minorities    Voting Rights Act of 1965│
└────────────────────────────────────────────────┘
```

C. _____ add new rights or extend the
    meaning of existing ones.

    1.   14th Amendment guarantees all citizens _____ .

    2.   24th Amendment forbade _____ which were
        used to deny voting rights.

> **Answers**
>
> *Constitutional Amendments*
> *equal protection*
> *poll taxes*

III. Struggles for equal rights.

  A. Women's rights.

    1.   19th and Early 20th Century: _____ movement
        (19th Amendment).

    2.   Late 20th Century: Equal _____ opportunities
        and sex discrimination.

  B. Minorities.

    1.   Racial Discrimination in the South: _____ .

    2.   The Civil Rights Movement: Equal voting rights, economic
        opportunity, and _____ .

> **Answers**
>
> *employment*   *Jim Crow laws*
> *equal justice*   *suffrage*

4. Citizen Participation And Responsibility

Study the following outline. Choose the correct item from the list of terms below to fill in the blanks.

I. Democracy depends on participation.

   A. United States is an indirect democracy or _____ .

   B. Main decisions made by _____ .

   C. Citizens' responsibilities: _____ representatives.

   D. _____ expanded: 15th, 19th, & 26th Amendments.

> **Answers**
>
> elected representatives   vote and monitor
> republic   voting rights

II. Paths to Participation

   A. Lobbies: focus on _____ .

   B. Political parties: represent variety of _____ .

     1. Choose candidates for office _____ .

     2. Raise money and supply workers for _____ .

   C. Third parties: focus on _____ .

> **Answers**
>
> campaigns   primaries and conventions
> major issues   special interests
> minority issues

III. Financial Responsibility: Paying Taxes.

   A. _____ for government programs.

   B. Types of taxes:

     1. _____ provide Federal, state, and local revenue.

     2. Sales and Property taxes provide _____ and local revenue.

     3. _____ taxes produce Federal revenue.

   C. When taxes aren't enough _____ create problems.

> **Answers**
>
> budget deficits   revenues   Social Security
> income taxes   state

5. Industrial And Technological Growth

Fill in the blank sections of the chart with the correct number choice.

Term	Definition	Significance
1.	post 1865 period in the USA when industry developed rapidly and a number of changes occurred as a result	America became a world industrial power
2. Immigration	vast numbers of foreign settlers arrived in the U.S.	
3. Laissez-faire		allowed unchecked growth of industry and investment
4.	large scale, rapid growth of cities	provided centers of industry and major markets for goods
5. Monopolies		provides for some efficiency and large scale production, but kills competition, causes price and quality dictatorship
6. Unions	workers' groups designed to bargain for wages, benefits, and safer working conditions	
7.	political groups formed to speak out for groups being hurt or exploited by industrial system	major parties so dominated by wealthy industrial groups that they did not respond to middle and lower class needs

---

Answers

1.   dominance of an industry by one company
2.   Industrial Revolution
3.   late 19th century government economic policy which minimized government regulation of business
4.   Populist / Progressive Parties
5.   provided the labor force needed in factories
6.   urbanization
7.   workers banned together to bargain and take collective action against power of wealthy industrial owners

6. Government Economic Policies

Fill in the chart using information at the left side of the chart.

Relationship	Policy	Change in Relationship
Government and market competition	In the Progressive Era, Presidents _____ used _____ (Sherman and Clayton Acts) to prosecute gigantic monopolies such as Morgan's _____ and Rockefeller's _____ to keep competition open in the market.	Government previously had a _____ approach to business, allowing each company to compete any way it wished.
Government and consumers	In response to the farmers' problems with the railroads in the late 19th Century, the federal government passed the _____ (1887). It stated "all charges... shall be fair and reasonable." It regulated the railroads by prohibiting pools, rebates, high rates for short hauls, and rate discrimination.	When the Federal Government created the Interstate Commerce Commission to investigate unfair treatment of railroad customers, it established a new role of _____ .
Government and workers	The Fair Labor Standards Act (1938) passed in the New Deal Era created _____ and rules on _____ maximum working hours.	The Federal Government created protection for workers against _____ by _____ unscrupulous employers.

Answers

antitrust laws

exploitation

Interstate Commerce Act

laissez-faire

minimum wages

Northern Securities Company

regulator of business

Roosevelt, Taft, Wilson

Standard Oil Company

7. Foreign Policy

Complete both the outline and the chart by using the words at the end of the assignment on the next page.

I. U.S. Imperialism [1890-1914] (*Answers at bottom of pg. 113*)

    A. Causes:

        1. Provide new sources of _____ materials for industry.

        2. Establish overseas _____ posts.

        3. Spread _____ religion.

    B. Actions Taken:

        1. Control of Cuba, _____ , Puerto Rico and _____ .

        2. Through the Open door Policy, trading rights in _____ .

II. Isolation and Global Involvement [1914-1945]

    (*Answers at bottom of pg. 113*)

World War I	Isolation Period	World War II
Cause: Submarine warfare by _____	Senate _____ Versailles Treaty and League of Nations	Lend-_____ Act
War Aims: Wilson's _____ Points	_____ Acts of the 1930's	Japan's Attack on _____ Harbor
Peace: Treaty of _____ and League of _____		U.S. drops _____ bomb on Hiroshima _____ Nations created

III. Post World War II [1945-present] (*Answers at bottom of page*)

A. _____ of Communism:

    1.   To strengthen war-torn Europe's Economy: _____ Plan

    2.   Aid countries fighting communism: _____ Doctrine

    3.   Military Defense Alliance: _____ .

    4.   Containment Actions: _____ and _____ .

B. Diplomatic Dealing With the Soviets:

    1.   1960's: _____ Test Ban Treaty.

    2.   1970's: Nixon's policy of _____ .

    3.   1980's: End of _____ War.

C. Preserving Self-Interest:

    1.   Trade agreements to increase _____ .

    2.   Promoting peace and stability in the Middle _____ .

Part I. Answers

raw	*trading*	*Christian*
Philippines	*Guam*	*China*

Part II. Answers

atomic	*lease*	*rejects*
fourteen	*Nations*	*United*
Germany	*Neutrality*	*Versailles*
	Pearl	

Part III. Answers

Cold	*exports*	*N.A.T.O.*
Containment	*Korea*	*Nuclear*
Détente	*Marshall*	*Truman*
East		*Vietnam*

8. Contemporary Issues

I.   Economic Issues: (Choose the *correct word*)

A.   The Federal deficit grows when the government spends _____ than it collects. (*more / less*)

B.   The budget deficit continues to be a problem because elected officials do not like to_____ taxes. (*increase / decrease*)

C.   Federal income tax rates go up for those with _____ incomes. (*higher / lower*)

II. Social Issues: (unscramble the **boldfaced words**)

A.   The elderly are concerned that the (**SALOIC CRITUYES**) _____ _____ and (**DEACRIME**) _____ systems are riddled with problems.

B.   Major public health concerns include: (**SAID**) _____ and (**RUGD SUABE**) _____ _____.

C.   Disturbing signs of poverty include:
Rising (**PTOLEMYMUENN**) _____ and
(**LESSONMESSHE**) _____.

III. Global Issues: (Change the **boldfaced words** to make the statements true.)

A.   The trade (**surplus**) _____ is caused by the percent of imports being greater than the percent of exports.

B.   Increased trade in the modern world for commodities such as oil has led to greater (**independence**) _____ of nations.

C.   The United States is concerned about violations of human rights especially the apartheid policies of the (**Middle East**) _____ _____.

Keys To Review

Appendices

The following pages contain reference lists, charts, and maps related to the eight study themes presented in this book. Checking this reference material is useful when you are doing the theme reading or looking for factual evidence when writing practice essays.

It is common to base Competency Test essays on ideas such as those on the **"13 Enduring Issues"** chart on pages 116-117. Test writers often use the 13 Issues when developing questions. To use the chart, cover the "Explanation" and "Examples" columns and see if you can explain them in your own words to yourself or a study partner.

The **"Summary of the United States Constitution"** on pages 118-119 gives you a concise outline to help whenever reference is made to the Constitution in the study lessons.

The three **"Key Actions"** charts on pages 120-125 (including the Congress, President, and Supreme Court) show historic examples of the range and variety of matters dealt with by the branches of the Federal Government. Use these facts when writing answers on government essay questions.

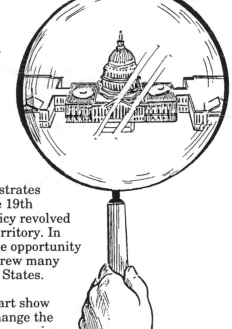

Questions related to the **"reference maps"** on pages 126 and 127 appear periodically. The **Territorial Map** illustrates how rapidly the nation expanded in the 19th Century. Much of our early foreign policy revolved around wars and treaties that added territory. In addition, the map is a reminder that the opportunity offered by this vast expansion of land drew many thousands of immigrants to the United States.

The **Electoral College Map** and chart show how the recent population shifts will change the Congressional power structure and the campaigns for the presidency in the future.

As much as 30 percent of typical U.S. History and Government Competency Test questions deal with government. When making your final preparation for the test, it is worth reviewing these appendices.

13 Enduring Issues

Issue	Explanation	Example of Enduring Issue
1. National Power: limits and potentials	Increases or decreases in the amount of power the Federal Government exercises.	• Attempts to settle slavery issue by compromise (1820-1860) • Federal power in the Great Depression • L. B. Johnson and the Great Society (1964-1969)
2. Federalism: the balance between nation and state	Federalism is the system of power being divided and shared among a strong central government and the 50 states.	• Power over interstate commerce: *Munn v. Illinois* (1876), Interstate Commerce Act (1887) • School Desegregation: *Brown v. Bd. of Ed.* (1954), Montgomery Boycott (1955) • Reagan's "New Federalism" (1980's)
3. Judiciary: interpreter of Constitution or shaper of public policy	Supreme Court has a role in broadening governmental power.	• *Marbury v. Madison (1803), McCulloch v. Maryland (1819)* • Dred Scott Decision (1857) • *Brown v. Bd. of Ed.* (1954)
4. Civil Liberties: the balance between the government and the individual	Basic national civil liberties are found in Bill of Rights and applied to states under the 14th Amendment. The courts have modified and reinterpreted them.	• Clear and present danger rule: *Schenck v. United States* (1919) *Korematsu v. United States* (1943)
5. Rights of the Accused and Protection of the Community	Individual rights in arrest and trial situations are found in the Bill of Rights.	• *Gideon v. Wainwright* (1962) *Miranda v. Arizona* (1966)
6. Equality: its definition as a Constitutional value	14th Amendment guarantees "equal protection of the laws" to all citizens.	• Civil Rights Movement (1950-70) • Native-American search for equality (1960's-1970's)

13 Enduring Issues

Issue	Explanation	Example of Enduring Issue
7. Rights of Women under the Constitution	Legal status of women has changed as a result of laws and amendments.	• Suffrage Movement and the 19th Amendment • Women's Liberation Movement and struggle for equal rights
8. Rights of Ethnic and Racial Groups under the Constitution	Minorities struggle against inequality because of uneven interpretations of the 14th Amendment.	• Nativism and Immigrants • Civil Disobedience and Dr. King
9. Presidential Power in Wartime and Foreign Affairs	Executive power grew as America's role in the world changed.	• Wilson: World War I and Versailles • FDR: Edging into World War II and Summit diplomacy • Johnson, Nixon, and Vietnam
10. Separation of Powers and the Capacity to Govern	Relationship of three branches is in constant change.	• Congressional and Presidential rivalry over Reconstruction • FDR and Court Packing • Nixon and Watergate • Reagan and Iran-Contra
11. Avenues of Representation	Continuing expansion of American democracy through the amendments and voting rights legislation.	• Direct election for U.S. Senators • Expansion of suffrage for blacks, women, and youth
12. Property Rights and Economic Policy	Economic function of government is public welfare v. accumulation of private wealth.	• Hamilton's policies and financial structure • Government control of business: anti-trust acts and consumer protection • Social Security, labor rights, and deficit spending • Supply-side economic policies under Reagan
13. Constitutional Change and Flexibility	Capacity of American government to deal with new situations.	• "Elastic Clause" in operation • "Unwritten Constitution:" political parties and Cabinet • Judicial Review and key precedents

Summary:

The United States Constitution

Preamble

We the people of the United States, in order to form a more perfect union, establish justice, insure domestic tranquility, provide for the common defense, promote the general welfare, and secure the blessings of liberty for ourselves and our posterity, do ordain and establish this Constitution of the United States of America.

Original Constitution

Article I:	Establishes Congress as a bicameral legislative branch (House of Rep. & Senate); how members are chosen and terms; lists 17 specific powers plus the "elastic clause;" presidential veto and override; actions prohibited
Article II:	Establishes executive branch with President and Vice-President; duties of office; how elected; appointment power; checks on power, including impeachment procedure
Article III:	Establishes judicial branch, with Supreme Court and its jurisdiction; how Congress sets up lower Federal courts; defines treason
Article IV:	Declares equality among the states, extradition, admission of new states, Congress' authority over territories; requires republican form of government in all states
Article V:	Establishes procedure for amending the Constitution
Article VI:	Declares Constitution the Supreme law of the land
Article VII:	Establishes procedure for the 13 states to ratify the new Constitution

First Ten Amendments

Bill of Rights (1791)

1st Amendment	- freedom of speech, press, assembly, and free exercise of religion
2nd Amendment	- right to bear arms
3rd Amendment	- forbids government from quartering of troops in peacetime
4th Amendment	- protects against unwarranted search
5th Amendment	- protects rights of accused by due process; eminent domain
6th Amendment	- protects rights to fair trial and counsel
7th Amendment	- right of jury trial in civil cases
8th Amendment	- protects against cruel punishment and excessive bail
9th Amendment	- rights not specifically mentioned still exist
10th Amendment	- powers not specified in Constitution left to states and people

Additional Amendments

11th Amendment (1795)	- suits by citizens of one state against a particular state must be heard in the latter's courts not in Federal courts
12th Amendment (1804)	- electors must use separate ballots for President and Vice-President
13th Amendment (1865)	- abolishes slavery
14th Amendment (1868)	- defines citizenship, application of due process and equal protection
15th Amendment (1870)	- defines citizens' right to vote
16th Amendment (1913)	- allows Federal income tax
17th Amendment (1913)	- direct popular election of U.S. Senators
18th Amendment (1919)	- manufacture, sale, importation, and transportation of alcoholic beverages forbidden in U.S. (repealed by 21st Amend.)
19th Amendment (1920)	- right of women to vote
20th Amendment (1933)	- redefines term of President & sessions of Congress
21st Amendment (1933)	- repeal of prohibition amendment (18th)
22nd Amendment (1951)	- limits Presidential terms
23rd Amendment (1961)	- provides presidential electors for District of Columbia
24th Amendment (1964)	- abolishes poll taxes in Federal elections
25th Amendment (1967)	- defines succession to Presidency and disability of President
26th Amendment (1971)	- eighteen year-old citizens may vote in Federal elections
27th Amendment (1992)	- sitting Congress may not raise its own salary

Key Congressional Actions

Government

Organization:

1789 State, Treasury, & War Depts. created
1867 Reconstruction Plan
1883 Civil Service Commission
1947 Presidential Succession Act

Individual

Rights Clarified:

1957 Civil Rights Commission created
1964 Civil Rights Act
1965 Voting Rights Act

Economic Life

Business Regulation:
1887 Interstate Commerce Act (railroads)
1890 Sherman Antitrust Act (monopoly)
1914 Clayton Antitrust Act (monopolies)
1914 Federal Trade Commission created (fair competition)
1934 Securities and Exchange Act commerce (stock regulation)

Working Conditions:
1935 National Labor Relations Act
1938 Fair Labor Standards Act
1947 Taft Hartley Act (control unions)
1962 Manpower Development Act (retrain workers)
1964 Equal Employment Opportunity Commission

Taxation:
1832 Tariff of Abominations
1913 Underwood Tariff
1928 Hawley-Smoot Tariff
1986 Comprehensive Tax Reform Law

Banking:
1791 Bank of U.S. chartered (rechartered 1816; vetoed 1832)
1913 Federal Reserve Act (control banks & money supply)
1933 Federal Deposit Insurance Corporation created
1972 Truth-in Lending Act
1980 Depository Institution Deregulation Act
1989 Resolution Trust Corp. (Savings & Loan crisis)

Aid to Commerce:
1811 National Road begun
1903 Commerce and Labor Depts.
1979 Loan to save Chrysler Corp. ($1.5 billion)

Relief:
1933 "Hundred Days" New Deal legislation (depression)
1966 "War on Poverty" legislation

Consumer Protection:
1906 Meat Inspection Act
1906 Pure Food & Drug Act
1938 Food, Drug, & Cosmetic Act commerce-consumer protection
1972 Consumer Products Safety Commission

Key Congressional Actions

Social Action

Slavery:
1820 Missouri Compromise /
Compromise of 1850 /
Freedman's Bureau (1865)

Education:
1862 Morill Act (land-grant
colleges)
1917 Smith-Hughes Act
(vocational schools)
1965 Elementary and Secondary
Education Act

Elderly:
1935 Social Security Act (old age
pensions / survivors'
benefits)
1965 Medicare Act

Living Conditions:
1862 Homestead Act
1961 Housing Act

Immigration:
1882 Chinese Exclusion Act
1921 Emergency Quota Act (also
1924)
1929 National Origins Act
1965 Immigration Act (abolished
1920's quotas)
1986 Immigration Reform &
Control Act

Indian Life:
1887 Dawes Act (reservations /
schools)
1934 Indian Reorganization Act

Environmental Protection:
1901 Newlands Act
(land conservation)
1970 Environmental Protection
Agency created

Foreign Affairs

Acts and Treaties:
1803 Louisiana Purchase
approved
1807 Embargo Act
1812 War Declared on Britain /
ratified Treaty of Ghent
(1814)
1818 Canada Boundary Treaty
1819 Florida Purchase approved
1846 Oregon Boundary Treaty
1846 War declared on Mexico
/ratified treaty with Mexico
(1848)
1898 War declared on Spain/
ratified Treaty of Paris
1898 Hawaii annexed
1903 Panama Canal Zone Treaty
ratified
1917 War declared on Germany
(WWI)
1917 Virgin Islands purchased
1919 Treaty of Versailles rejected
1928 Kellogg-Briand Treaty
ratified
1935 Neutrality Acts (also 1937 &
1939)
1941 Lend Lease Act
1941 War declared on Axis
(WWII)
1945 United Nations Treaty
approved
1946 Philippines granted
independence
1947 European Recovery Act
(Marshall Plan)
1949 NATO treaty approved
1973 Military draft ended
1973 War Powers Act (limits
President's military power)
1978 Treaty to return Panama
Canal Zone ratified

Key Presidential Actions

- ## George Washington (1789-1797)

  Organized government under new Constitution
  Stabilized economy
  Proclaimed neutral status in world affairs
  Set many precedents still followed today

- ## Thomas Jefferson (1801-1809)

  Leader of Party (Democratic-Republican)
  Used idea of implied power
  Louisiana purchased (territorial expansion)
  Lewis & Clark Expedition
  War with Barbary Pirates
  Trade embargo to avoid European war

- ## Abraham Lincoln (1861-1865)

  Crisis management (Civil War)
  Emancipation Proclamation

- ## William McKinley (1897-1901)

  Spanish-American War
  Imperial expansion (colonialism)

- ## Theodore Roosevelt (1901-1909)

  Forceful use of executive power to move Congress
  Added "Voice of the People" role
  Anti-trust campaigns
  Consumer protection
  Conservation program
  Panama Canal

- ## Woodrow Wilson (1913-1921)

  Increased use of power of Chief Legislator role
  Anti-trust campaign
  Banking regulation
  World War I leader
  Peace negotiator
  Helped create the League of Nations

Key Presidential Actions

- ## Franklin Roosevelt (1933-1945)

  New Deal legislative programs to combat the Great Depression
  Added "Manager of the Economy" role
  Business and financial regulations
  Workers' rights
  World War II leader
  Helped create the United Nations

- ## Harry Truman (1945-1953)

  World War II leader
  Aid to rebuild Europe
  Added "leader of the free world" role
  Cold War containment of communism
  NATO Alliance
  Korean War leader

- ## Lyndon Johnson (1963-1969)

  Great Society welfare reform programs
  Immigration reform
  Urban redevelopment
  Civil Rights acts
  Vietnam War leader

- ## Richard Nixon (1969-1974)

  Escalated then ended Vietnam War
  Détente with Red China / U.S.S.R.
  Watergate scandal led to first Presidential resignation

- ## Ronald Reagan (1981-1989)

  "Supply-Side" budget and tax reductions (Manager of Economy)
  Anti-communist invasions (Grenada, Costa Rica, Nicaragua)
  Deregulation of banks
  Anti-terrorist actions
  Troop and arms reduction treaties with U.S.S.R.
  Iran-Contra aid (struggle with Congress)

Key Supreme Court Actions

Issue	Case
1. Freedom of Speech	1. *Schenck v. United States (1919)*
2. Freedom of Religion	2. *Engel v. Vitale (1962)*
3. Death Penalty	3. *Gregg v. Georgia (1976)*
4a. Due Process Rights of Accused Persons	4a. *Gideon v. Wainwright (1963)*
4b. Due Process Rights of Accused Persons	4b. *Miranda v. Arizona (1966)*
5. Press Censorship	5. *New York Times v. United States (1972)*
6. Abortion	6. *Roe v. Wade (1973)*
7. Judicial Power	7. *Marbury v. Madison (1803)*
8. Monopolies	8. *Northern Securities Co. v. United States (1903)*
9a. Racial Segregation	9a. *Plessy v. Ferguson (1896)*
9b. Racial Segregation	9b. *Brown v. Board of Education of Topeka (1954)*
10. Slavery	10. *Dred Scott v. Sanford (1857)*
11. Presidential Power	11. *United States v. Nixon (1972)*

Key Supreme Court Actions

Decision

1. The Supreme Court said government could jail a socialist for encouraging soldiers not to fight during World War I. Individual freedom of speech could be suspended if there were a "clear and present danger" to society.

2. The Supreme Court declared a state could not require school children to say a specific prayer.

3. The Supreme Court said the Death penalty was appropriate for murder and rape. It does not violate the 8th Amendment as being cruel and unusual punishment.

4a. The Supreme Court said a state which refused to give legal counsel to a person accused of a crime violated the person's 6th Amendment right.

4b. The Supreme Court said a person must be clearly informed of all Constitutional due process rights. Police must now read all suspects being placed under arrest the "four-fold warning" advising them of their 5th and 6th Amendment rights.

5. The Supreme Court said newspapers could publish secret government documents they obtain under the 1st Amendment right of the people to be informed.

6. The Supreme Court said states cannot prevent women from having abortions during the first six months of pregnancy.

7. The Supreme Court rejected a 1789 Judiciary Act by Congress because it violated the principle of separation of power. For the first time, the Supreme Court declared a Federal law unconstitutional. The power of Federal judicial review of all laws in light of the Constitution was established.

8. The Supreme Court upheld the government's power under the Sherman Antitrust Act to stop monopolies from destroying free competition in the marketplace.

9a. The Supreme Court upheld "Jim Crow" segregation laws as fair as long as separate facilities for races were equal.

9b. The Supreme Court overturned Plessy decision. Segregation laws are unfair and unequal because they treat one group racial as inferior.

10. The Supreme Court tried to settle the slavery issue by declaring slaves were not citizens, but property and private property was protected by the Constitution.

11. The Supreme Court said the President's privilege to keep executive documents confidential was not absolute. Nixon was not immune from Congressional investigations. The Court ordered Nixon to turn over documents about his role in the Watergate scandal.

United States Territorial Expansion

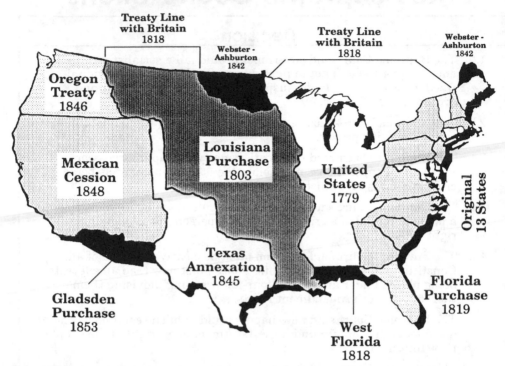

Louisiana (1803)	• Purchased from France for $15 million; Doubled U.S. territory, plus port of New Orleans
Northern Border (1818)	• Set western U.S. Canadian border as 49th parallel
Western Florida (1818)	• Treaty settled United States' claims on Spanish territory
Florida (1819)	• U.S. paid $5 million to Spain for rest of Florida Peninsula
Northern Maine (1842)	• Webster-Ashburton Treaty settled boundary with British
Texas (1845)	• Congress accepted the request of the independent Republic of Texas to be annexed
Oregon (1846)	• Treaty with Britain extended the 49th parallel boundary from the Rockies to the Pacific
Mexican Cession (1848)	• At end of War with Mexico, U.S. paid $15 million for huge south west region
Gadsden Purchase (1853)	• Purchased from Mexico to finish a transcontinental rail line

Electoral College

The number of Electoral College votes for each state is determined by adding the number of Representatives and Senators. To be elected President, a candidate needs 270 of the 538 votes. In the 1980's, there was a shift of population from the industrial Northeast to the South and West. The farm belt also lost in Congress. This major shift in representation is likely to change the political atmosphere in Washington D.C. for the 1990's. The economically conservative South and West have gained more Congressional seats.

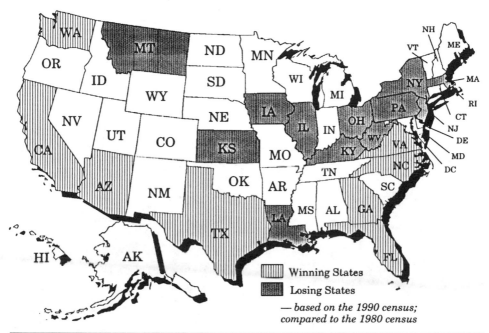

▨ Winning States

▨ Losing States

— based on the 1990 census;
compared to the 1980 census

Electoral College Votes

AL	Alabama	9	KY	Kentucky	8	ND	No Dakota	3
AK	Alaska	3	LA	Louisiana	9	OH	Ohio	21
AZ	Arizona	7	ME	Maine	4	OK	Oklahoma	8
AR	Arkansas	6	MD	Maryland	10	OR	Oregon	7
CA	California	54	MA	Massachusetts	12	PA	Pennsylvania	23
CO	Colorado	8	MI	Michigan	18	RI	Rhode Island	4
CT	Connecticut	8	MN	Minnesota	10	SC	So Carolina	8
DE	Delaware	3	MS	Mississippi	7	SD	So Dakota	3
DC	Washington D.C.	3	MO	Missouri	11	TN	Tennessee	11
FL	Florida	25	MT	Montana	3	TX	Texas	32
GA	Georgia	13	NE	Nebraska	5	UT	Utah	5
HI	Hawaii	4	NV	Nevada	4	VT	Vermont	3
ID	Idaho	4	NH	New Hampshire	4	VA	Virginia	13
IL	Illinois	22	NJ	New Jersey	15	WA	Washington	11
IN	Indiana	12	NM	New Mexico	5	WV	W. Virginia	5
IA	Iowa	7	NY	New York	33	WI	Wisconsin	11
KS	Kansas	6	NC	No Carolina	14	WY	Wyoming	3